Woman Invisible

6-95

CW00722808

WOMAN INVISIBLE

A Personal Odyssey In Christian Feminism

MARGA BÜHRIG

BURNS & OATES

First published in this translation in 1993
BURNS & OATES,
Wellwood, North Farm Road,
Tunbridge Wells, Kent TN2 3DR

Published originally in Germany in 1987 by
Kreuz Verlag, Stuttgart,
under the title *Die unsichtbare Frau und der Gott
der Väter: Eine Einführung in die feministische
Theologie*

ISBN: 0 86012 202 6

Composition by Genesis Typesetting, Laser Quay,
Rochester, Kent
Printed and bound in Great Britain by
Biddles Ltd, Guildford and King's Lynn

Contents

Introduction   7

1. "Women are Invisible": Methodological   15
   Considerations

2. Women, Bible, Tradition   36

3. Images of God – Women's Experiences of God   55

4. Woman – Nature – Spirit   79

5. Women for an Inclusive Church: 105
   We Women too are Church

6. Postscript *by Lavinia Byrne IBVM*   123

Introduction

WHAT IS feminist theology? This is what many women and men are asking. A fashionable phenomenon that will peter out at some time or other? An intellectual middle-class women's hobby? A special type of liberation theology? Quite a few people say that speaking simply of a women's theology, a theology of and for women, would at least indicate what was included in this concept, and ask what the point of creating this new word "feminist" is. I understand these questions. Many women, including me, had to come a long way before we realized that we need this expression. and it is a painful realization that the majority of church leaders and academics have difficulty in taking this theology seriously and in facing its challenges. In Switzerland there is still not a single chair in feminist theology. Temporary, short-term teaching appointments, a few posts for women research assistants, and lectures on the fringes of universities and seminaries are (still) all that is possible in the academic field. But then it must be said that the origins of feminist theology are not to be found in universities and colleges. The springs of experience are bubbling up outside them, in countless women's groups, women's courses, women's church services, women's forums; and, whatever these events may be called, women of every age and of different educational backgrounds and circumstances come together in them. However, this movement needs thorough reflection, and it also needs dialogue with "real" theology, which, unfortunately, is still a man's theology.

The text of this book consists of the lectures which I gave in the summer term of 1986 while engaged to lecture at the (Catholic) Faculty of Theology of Lucerne, under the title, "Women in Theology and the Church". This engagement forced me to review and set out in order my own experiences and what I have learned from the immense literature that has appeared in the English- and the German-speaking world. The following pages attempt to present some of the basic ideas which are important to me, and I hope thereby to bring about

7

a better understanding of what is meant by feminist theology.

"Woman Invisible in Church and Theology"

This was the title of the December 1985 issue of the international journal of theology, *Concilium*. At first sight this phrase seems absurd, since anybody who goes into a church finds women in the majority there. The picture changes, however, when we look at church leaders and the majority of ordained ministers, and, as stated above, of faculties of theology. Even the increasing number of Protestant women theologians who are working with equal rights in our congregations are moulded by a theology which accords them no recognition as women. Right from the outset, it was always men who "did" theology, and they passed judgment on the place and role of women. This can be seen much more clearly in Catholic and Orthodox churches, in fact everywhere where women are excluded from the priesthood. However, even in the Reformed tradition, where something is beginning to move, the basic problems have not been solved. Even the Reformed Churches have not overcome the domination of patriarchy, and women suddenly come up against barriers when they do not conform, or even worse, they are simply forgotten. Here are two examples of this, one from our own times and one from New Testament times:

1. In the World Council of Churches, they have been working for years on a study programme with the title, "The Community of Men and Women in the Church". It was brought to a conclusion with a large conference in Sheffield in 1981, and the World Assembly of the WCC in Vancouver (1983) recommended further study. However, the co-ordinator of the study, the American Constance Parvey, said in 1986: "Sheffield has been silenced – not forcibly silenced by any one person, but simply ignored by those who set priorities in the churches' theology and seminary education."[1] This is the way women became invisible.

---

1. *One World*, 113 (Geneva: WCC) March 1986, p.17.

2. But when and where did this process start? I do not want to put forward any speculations here about the origins of patriarchy, but much more simply, and perhaps unscientifically, to refer to very well-known things that I, incidentally, for many years of my life failed to notice myself. I recall the story of Easter. In all four Gospels it is reported that women were the first to go to Jesus' tomb. The reports differ from each other in details. The abiding fact is that women – or *one* woman in John's Gospel – were the first to hear the message of the resurrection and to receive the commission to spread it abroad. They were to take the Good News to the disciples. Mark reports that they did not do this because they were afraid; Luke recounts that the disciples did not believe them, but then immediately afterwards it is related how the Risen Christ appeared to two disciples, and they were not believed either. John deliberately tells the story in a completely different way. He describes the encounter between the Risen Christ and Mary Magdalene, who recognized him only when he called her by name. In all four Gospels women are found at the beginning of the encounters with the Risen Christ. So it is all the more amazing that in the First Letter of the Apostle Paul to the Corinthians (15:3ff) we do not find the women in the list of witnesses to the resurrection. Peter is named first, then the Twelve, then "more than five hundred brethren", then James, then all the Apostles, then finally Paul himself. The women are completely forgotten. Right up to the present they do not appear in any Easter church liturgy.

Women want to be seen and heard

Nowadays, more and more women are aware of such things. They perceive their second-class status, they are indignant that women – both in the Bible and still today – in spite of all assertions to the contrary, are still not really given equal status. Scholars such as Elisabeth Schüssler Fiorenza have researched with academic precision and found traces of this. She speaks of the first community, the Jesus movement, as a fellowship of men and women with equal rights, of mutuality and friendship, with no separation brought about by one person being set over the others. This community of practical (and not only theoretical) equals, who were not dependent upon each other, has been lost in our churches. In the introduction to the German edition of the ecumenical study mentioned above, Bärbel von Wartenberg writes:

> In the majority of churches of the German Evangelical Church (E.K.D.) we have achieved the formal equality of women and men; but we are a long way from dealing with what it means to allow women and men to be full and equal representatives of the Church, as a question of our inner attitudes. Women are looking for a new language, a new expression, new ways of thinking theologically, which are of importance for the whole Church – but they often do this on the margins of the Church. The criticism of church orders, doctrinal systems and procedures in Church and society created by men points towards something like a "Coperni-can Revolution", which is, slowly at first, becoming visible in all its dimensions.[2]

So the so-called "women's question" deals not only with the injury done to the human rights of women, but with the life of the Church, which cannot be *whole* without the (greater) half of humanity, or more precisely of believers. The "Copernican Revolution" would be a re-organization of the Church from the bottom upwards, a renewal under new conditions, an overcoming of patriarchy. That is, perhaps, Utopia. It could, however, also be a question of survival for the Church. Because such basic questions are involved, the term "theology of women" is inadequate.

Why so late?

This question is more than justified: why have Christian women not seen and defined these problems much earlier? Women have had bibles and read them for long enough. They have been loyal members of the Church and have patiently let themselves be called to "brotherly love". Women have also defended themselves against the misuse of biblical texts in

---

2. *The Community of Women and Men in the Church*, ed. Constance C. Parvey (Grand Rapids: Eerdmans; Geneva: WCC, 1983).

political disputes. I recall the struggles over the ecclesiastical and political right of women to vote and to be elected, and in this connection, how often men, and even women, have used Paul's words from 1 Corinthians 14:34, "Let your women be silent in the congregation", or, in the abbreviated form of the Vulgate, "Let *the* woman be silent in the congregation", as an argument against the right of women to vote. Biblical texts as weapons in the hands of people who otherwise take little notice of the Bible! Many of us, including myself, have defended ourselves at the level of theological argument, and have tried to prove that this interpretation was false, and that these texts could not be used in this way in an entirely different situation. We have hoped and trusted that better insights would and could, of themselves as it were, change the situation. We have failed to see that paying no heed to women is more deeply rooted, and is more firmly anchored in the structures of our churches and our society than we realized.

The women's movement, whose origin did not lie within the churches and whose development in many ways bypassed the churches, has had a decisive influence in changing the behaviour of women. Its beginnings go right back to the French Revolution – I am thinking of the "Charter of the rights of women" of Olympe de Gouges. In the late nineteenth century and in the first two thirds of the twentieth it led to struggles for the admission of women to universities and other places of higher education, against prostitution and economic exploitation, for vocational training and opportunities, and finally for the political rights of women. This all took place, however, within the existing civic order. It was only the second wave of the women's movement after 1968, especially in the early 1970s, that produced the onset of radical criticism. If women, and in particular Christian women, had thought that now at last the hour of partnership, of the division of roles between men and women on an equal footing, had come, a new generation made further claims. Young women were disappointed that even in so-called progressive or alternative movements the old roles had not changed. They also discovered the significance of sexuality, and they began to struggle against the fact that their own female needs were not

taken seriously, let alone satisfied. They began to ask why only
men took decisions about war and peace, and also about the
right to abortion. Women banded together, often to the rage
and scorn of men. They discovered that "women together are
strong", or they could be, and also how much women meant
to each other, how much they could learn from each other.

Even when Christian women had trouble with many of
these claims, which can only be very roughly sketched out
here, this movement left its mark. Church women discovered
their dependence on male language and theology. They began
to get together in women's groups; they read the Bible
together; in their thirst for knowledge, they turned to biblical
figures of women with affection, and made their own
discoveries. They created their own space, because they
needed time to discover themselves. A German manifesto of
1972 stated:

> Women organize themselves separately, because one day it
> strikes them that society is and has been actively controlled
> by men, so that we must examine society and its institutions
> from the different standpoints of women, in order to
> participate actively in the shaping of our lives and our
> future.[3]

The word "society" could be replaced with "the church"
throughout. At any rate, the effects were both positive and
negative for Christian women. Positive, in that they experienced in their groups something of the liberating power of the
Gospel, in that they discovered how long-crippled or excised
powers of love and faith could be set free. Negative, because
they had to wrestle with the question of guilt more intensely
than women who had no connection with the Church – was it
not a sin to revolt against the sanctified, God-given orders, e.g.
marriage as the basic condition of human relations? – and
because they had to deal with an institution with which they
were emotionally involved: "We still love our church."

---

3. Herrad Schenk, *Die feministiche Herausforderung* (Munich: C.H. Beck, 1981),
p.116.

Feminist theology as liberation theology

At the conclusion of this introduction I must go back again to the terms "feminism" and "feminist theology". The term "feminism" came into being in the more recent women's movement. It expresses the idea that the equal status of men and women is not enough, i.e. that this is completely impossible in a society in which men occupy all the important positions, and thereby have all the power to make decisions. Women call themselves feminists when they cannot and will not accept this status quo, when they liberate themselves (or try to liberate themselves) inwardly and then more and more outwardly from old states of dependence. Feminist theology means reflecting on and understanding this process in the framework of the biblical message. Catharina Halkes, one of the European "mothers" of feminist theology, writes in her book *Gott hat nicht nur starke Söhne*:

> On their way towards the dawning of their consciousness
> ... women experience transcendence, when they break the
> chains that bind them. In this way, they enter into a new
> space, where they throw their arms into the air, lift high their
> heads, and can cry aloud: "Here I am, I can be what I am
> ..." The experience of being valued as a human being is a
> fundamental experience that has to do with the roots of our
> being. Accepting and affirming one's own self can become
> the conditions or the fertile ground of a more adult attitude
> of faith.[4]

It is clear from this that feminist theology is a theology based on experience, and, in particular, the common experience of many women who are aware of their situation of dependence and oppression and "invisibility". It is tied up with specific historical situations. This is why the expression "theology of women" is not appropriate. It does not concern all women, but women in a particular situation. There is therefore no unifying system of theology in feminist theology. Feminist theology in

---

4. Catharina J.M. Halkes, *Gott hat nicht nür starke Söhne: Grundzüge einer feministische Theologie* (Siebenstern: Gütersloher Taschenbücher, 1971). p.33.

Africa and Asia, for example, differs in its appearance from that of Europe and North America, but nevertheless shares many common traits.

In recent years women from many places have begun to celebrate their own experiences of life and faith with each other. They have become liberated from the naked struggle "against" the old church structures, to strive "for", and in celebration "of" life. The love of life, which is God's gift, increasingly finds expression. In Zurich the church services held monthly by women are called "women's celebrations". The important thing about this is that this love includes everyone else who seeks or needs liberation, groups of the oppressed and minorities, just as much as children and men. They also need liberation from dependence. Feminists, both men and women, believe that women nowadays play a central role in this process of liberation.

Marga Bührig
Binningen, Autumn 1990

Chapter 1

"Women are Invisible": Methodological Considerations

ONE CAN tackle the subject of "Women in Church and theology" in very different ways. One can, for example, go back to the great female figures of the past, follow their footsteps, and so trace something like the path of women through the centuries. The only major difficulty with this is that there are relatively few women, and, moreover, only a particular kind of woman, who emerge in this way: women who have become prominent in some area and who have become well known, I am tempted to say, in spite of the fact that they were women. I think it is very important to investigate the lives and destinies of such women, but when we do that we must keep an aim in view. We must work out beforehand the criteria by which we wish to investigate these paths. From where should we derive these criteria? Should I try to make it clear that at certain points in history – in this case, church history – women were just as good as men (and in so doing, I would have taken men as the norm); or should I, on the contrary, throw light on the different nature of female piety and female thinking seen in these characters? By doing that, I would run the risk of reinforcing the existing stereotypes of what is masculine and what is feminine. One thing, at any rate, is certain: I would have to make it clear which criteria I was adopting in my enquiry and presentation, and only when I was in possession of these criteria would I be able to do that. There are many ways of attempting this nowadays. This is always the case when women themselves set about enquiring into their history. For this reason, the enquiry appears to me to be very meaningful, and also justified. I shall certainly use historical female characters in the course of this book, but they should not form the main part of my consideration.

Another possibility would be to investigate what others have thought about women: what, for example, theologians and Church Fathers have said and thought about women. However, the above considerations apply here as well, and, moreover, in this undertaking one fact must be given full weight: those who have thought about women, from the time of Paul the Apostle and the other authors of the New Testament writings onwards, have been men. Now it is undoubtedly interesting and necessary to make oneself familiar with these concepts; they tell us something about ourselves as well as about those who have developed them, but, as a contemporary woman and a theologian, I should not like to rely on the validity of these statements. In the ecumenical movement I have learned that I can understand the theology of Africans, Asians, and Latin Americans only if I listen to them speaking themselves, and that I should not look at them through the spectacles of my own church tradition and history. Naturally that applies also to texts from the past. Here also we have learned to ask under what conditions, with what objectives, and in whose interests the authors wrote these texts. However, I can really only apply this method when I have, as far as I possibly can, listened to the voices of those concerned, in this case the voices of women. I want initially to refrain from disputing masculine conceptions of what women are or should be. Naturally, it will not be possible to maintain this position in the long run.

After excluding both these possibilities, I find myself in a great state of embarrassment. I want to express this in the words of the title of the December 1985 issue of the journal *Concilium*: "Woman invisible in Church and Theology". How can I make the invisible visible? How can I give a voice to the dumb, those who have been rendered speechless, or have been silenced? However, first of all, I want to take issue with the phenomenon of our invisibility. At first glance, as we saw in the Introduction, this seems a paradox. Anybody who attends a church service, probably in most parts of the world, will see women everywhere, more women than men attending services, and partaking of the sacrament. They are therefore not invisible, they are easily seen, and without them there would presumably be many empty church pews. But the assertion that women are invisible does not refer to this very simple fact. To quote Constance Parvey again:

> Sheffield [where the final conference of the WCC Study on "The Community of Women and Men in the Church" took place] has been silenced . . . not forcibly silenced by any one person, but simply ignored by those who set priorities in the churches' theology and seminary education . . . Where have male theologians – and in particular Faith and Order constituents – used the Study as part of courses in ecclesiology or sacramental theology?[1]

The study was made in collaboration between the Women's Department and the powerful Faith and Order Commission, and adopted with great acclaim. At the World Assembly of the WCC in Vancouver in 1983, the promise was made that it would be continued and widely used, but in a very short time it disappeared. Naturally it is on sale in all the appropriate bookshops and it will also be in the stock of libraries in most theological colleges. But what is the use of that if it is not used? The result: "Women remain invisible."

In the same issue of *Concilium*, Elisabeth Schüssler Fiorenza describes this state of invisibility in greater detail. She refers to the well-known Pauline texts, that women should be silent in the congregation (1 Cor. 14:34–5; 1 Tim. 2:1–15), and then continues:

> To quote these well-worn biblical phrases again might be for some readers like pouring water into the Tiber or the Charles river. Yet women's theological silence in the Church is still reinforced. As recently as last May during a visit of Pope John Paul II to the Netherlands, Professor Catharina Halkes, the leading Roman Catholic feminist theologian in Europe, was forbidden to address the pontiff. Although

---

1. *One World* No 113 (Geneva: WCC), March 1986, p.17.

women can study theology, we can only rarely become professors at influential schools and faculties.

Elisabeth Gössmann, now Professor of "Christian Studies" at a Japanese university, after successfully completing her "Habilitation" [a thesis and trial lecture which qualifies one for appointment as professor in German universities. TRANS.], applied in vain for a chair in seventeen different European universities, although the qualification she has is uncontested. The last institute of higher education to reject her gave her age as justification for doing so.

To return to Elisabeth Schüssler Fiorenza. She establishes that nowhere do women, or women theologians, participate in the "magisterium" of the Church, that they are never called upon as experts, that their theological work does not appear in manuals of theology, and is not brought up in discussions. She concludes these remarks with the especially distressing statement that even liberation theologians do not pay attention to women. Finally on this point, a few more sentences from her:

> This deliberate or unconscious silencing of women in the Church engenders our ecclesiastical and theological invisibility. Although women are the majority of people still going to church and of those joining religious orders, the Church is officially represented by males only. Although the Church is called "our mother" and referred to by the pronoun "she", it is personified and governed by fathers and brothers only. Therefore, whenever we speak of the Church, we see before our eyes the pope in Rome, bishops or pastors, cardinals and monsignors, deacons and altar boys, all of whom are men.[2]

Protestants, it is true, cannot say the same about their own churches, but it is also the case with them that changes proceed very slowly, and the "higher up" we go in these churches, the fewer women we find there. And the problems generally go

---

2. *Concilium* 182, Dec. 1985.

much deeper than the mere question of numerical representation, as I shall show in the course of this exposition. At least in these churches "brotherliness" is more strongly represented, at least verbally – and the sisters should always understand themselves to be included therein ... But when I have to listen in every sermon to the fact that it is precisely as a Christian that a man (never a woman), must show brotherly love, or when preachers always speak of the God of our Fathers, as if there had never been mothers of the faith as well, then I experience exactly the same feeling as that which Elisabeth Schüssler Fiorenza describes. This may be a minor matter (and this is often said), but I am convinced that our language gives away more of our real moral concepts and well-established societal and ecclesiastical structures than we would like. Many women have become sensitive to exclusive language. Many of us, however, have also realized for how long we did not jib at these expressions ourselves, how we even used them ourselves. Reading through many old texts of mine in connection with a book I am writing, I realized that I used to speak in exactly the same way, and I have had to begin to re-educate myself in recent years. Even we women have been socially conditioned in androcentric ways of thinking.

So I have decided to take this fact, which I have provisionally called "the invisibility of women" as the starting point of my reflections. In my opinion, it should not be played down, but must be made the basis, the starting point, of everything that follows. If we turn away from it too quickly and disregard it, we can of course produce very beautiful theories about the nature or the gifts or the service of women, but these exist in a vacuum, as it were, and bear no relation to reality.

In order to define and justify my starting point somewhat better, I should like to develop two ideas a little further. Elisabeth Schüssler Fiorenza says in the passage already quoted:

Women as Church are invisible neither by accident nor by our own default but by patriarchal law that excludes us from church office on the basis of sex ... In short, my thesis is: the silence and invisibility of women is generated by the patriarchal structures of the Church and maintained by androcentric, i.e. male-defined theology.[3]

In practice, this means that women do not appear as subjects in the Church and theology, even if it may seem so, but always in a place assigned to them and in a role that is expected of them. Now that applies within patriarchy even to men; for example, one could speak similarly of the so-called laity, both men and women, but the difference remains that women, even when there are other relationships of superiority and inferiority, remain in second place in relation to men. In a certain sense they are objects, not subjects acting on their own initiative.

So when did this start? As I said briefly in the Introduction, I do not want to speculate at this point about the origins of patriarchy, but in a simpler and perhaps less scientific manner I want to examine some very well-known events, which, for many years of my life, I must admit, I failed to notice. I should like to remind you of the Easter story. In all four Gospels it is reported that women were the first to go to Jesus' tomb. The reports differ, but only in details which have nothing to do with the matter in hand. Even the names of the women do not completely agree, except for one who is named in all accounts, namely Mary from Magdala, known in our tradition as Mary Magdalene. The name of the place, her place of origin, has become her own name. Women, or a woman, were the first to receive the message of the resurrection: the Risen Christ himself meets them, or angels communicate to them the news of his resurrection; they are to take the good news to the disciples. Mark reports that they did not do this because they were afraid; Luke relates that the disciples did not believe them, and in Matthew it is also said that the disciples did not believe them, but immediately afterwards that the Risen Christ appeared to two disciples, and that they were not believed either. It is well known that John tells the story quite differently. He describes the encounter between the Risen Christ and Mary Magdalene, who recognized him only when

---

3. *Ibid.*

he called her by name. But still, in all four Evangelists women are present at the start of the encounters with the Risen Christ. So it is all the more amazing that in the First Letter of Paul to the Corinthians, in chapter 15, which deals with the resurrection of Christ and the resurrection of the dead, we no longer find women in the list of the first witnesses to the Resurrection. Now, 1 Corinthians is older than the Gospels. The Gospel of Mark appeared about 70CE, 1 Corinthians about 20 years earlier. Paul cannot then have known the story in the form in which we know it today. He knew for sure however the oral tradition, and the women were definitely not missing from that. But he gives the following first witnesses in 1 Corinthians 15:3ff:

> For I delivered to you as of first importance what I also received, that Christ died for our sins in accordance with the scriptures, that he was buried, and that he was raised again on the third day in accordance with the scriptures, and that he appeared to Cephas, then to the Twelve. Then he appeared to more than 500 brethren at one time most of whom are still alive though some have fallen asleep. Then he appeared to James, then to all the Apostles. Last of all as to one untimely born, he appeared also to me.[4]

In various Protestant commentaries and Karl Barth's "The Resurrection of the Dead", I have read explanations of this passage. Neither Barth nor any of the other (male) authors who make so many comments about the significance of this passage, and who also make comparisons between the reports of the Evangelists and Paul's exposition, makes the slightest reference to the fact that the women have been left out here. For Karl Barth it is clear anyway that only one thing is important in this passage, namely that Christ is risen. For him it is a matter of complete indifference who is mentioned here.

---

4. Except where otherwise stated, all scriptural translations are from the Revised Standard Version. The author, when not using her own translation from the original Greek, uses a Swisss Reformed version, not the German Luther Bible or its linear successors [TRANS].

He is also not concerned with exegesis, but with dogmatic theology. Exegetical scholars work carefully with this narrative, but nevertheless do not hit upon the idea that the women have been left out. However, when Heinz Dietrich Wendland (who has stood out passionately for the ministry of women and for their equality in the Church) states that this enumeration is a list of the unique "Church-founding" Easter appearances, one must indeed then ask whether it is of so little importance that the women have been forgotten at precisely the point which deals with the experiences on which the Church is founded. Women have a place where it is a matter of encounters and living faith, but just as in public life, so too in the public life of the Church, they were not credible witnesses. That has always proved to be the case in the course of history. Many women today are hurt that the women are absent here, and one can begin to picture how the history of the Church would have unfolded, if Paul had not overlooked them, forgotten them, if he had at least mentioned them. But they have already been rendered invisible at the very outset of the history of the Christian Church.

Yet apart from what present-day women want, there is more recent serious research by both men and women on this subject. Some of it has been known for a long time, but just as little notice has been taken of it as the "forgotten" reports to which reference has already been made. It hinges on the significance of Mary Magdalene in various so-called Apocryphal Gospels. We have all probably at one time learned that the canon of scripture is a divinely-inspired exclusive collection of writings, forever valid, through which the Word of God is transmitted to us by the Spirit. Nevertheless, research has been intensively conducted into the extra-canonical writings which have been preserved only in fragments. This has given us a picture of a situation where the texts that have been elevated into the canon formed part of a much wider living tradition, and through the serious disputes and struggles of different groups, reached the position that they have today in all Christian churches. The interesting thing in all this is the observation that in individual writings women played a more significant role than in the canonical scriptures. So in the *Pistis*

Sophia,[5] in a discussion between Jesus and the disciples and the "holy women" we read: "But Maria the Magdalene and John the Virgin will become excelling above all my disciples, and all men who will receive the Mystery of the Ineffable, they will become on my left and on my right...." Here Mary Magdalene is accorded the first place, (together with John the Beloved Disciple), and not Peter. The *Pistis Sophia* belongs to a Gnostic tradition, not to the orthodox line which stands behind the present established canon.

A passage from the *Gospel of Mary* points in the same direction.[6] It is narrated here that the disciples mourned Jesus' death and feared for their lives. Mary Magdalene stands up and encourages them with these words: "Do not weep and moan, and have no doubts, since his grace will be with you all and will protect you." Peter demands that Mary tell them what words of Jesus she remembers. To everyone's surprise, she does not speak of the past, but refers to a vision that she has had, that is, to a continuing revelation of Jesus. Andrew, one of the disciples, casts doubt on this statement, and Peter agrees with him. He laughs at Mary Magdalene, and doubts that she has really seen Jesus and heard him. Then the narrative continues: "Mary wept and spoke to Peter: 'My brother Peter, what do you believe then? Do you believe that I am lying about the Redeemer?' Levi interrupted and spoke to Peter: 'Peter, you have always been quick-tempered ... If the Redeemer has made her worthy, who are you then to reject her?'"

The argument of Elisabeth Schüssler Fiorenza and Elaine Pagels runs as follows: up until the third and fourth centuries there were congregations in which Mary Magdalene was the first and crucial witness to the Resurrection, and there were "orthodox" congregations in which Peter took on this role, and which furthermore drew up a list of men who were witnesses to the Resurrection (cf. 1 Cor. 15). This list was final.

---

5. *Pistis Sophia,* a literal translation from the Coptic by George Horner (London: SPCK, 1924), second document, v. 215b, here p.116.
6. Elaine Pagels, *The Gnostic Gospels* London: Wiedenfeld and Nicholson, 1980), p.13.

The Church based its authority on the testimony of these men, whose experience was unrepeatable, since it is only in the succession to them, (or at any rate in believing acceptance of their testimony), that the authority of the true Church rests. The story is different among the followers of Mary Magdalene. Remember the passage from the *Pistis Sophia*: "All men who receive the Mystery of the Ineffable will become on my right hand and on my left." This means that, beyond a certain circle, genuine experience of God – I even dare to say: revelation of the Risen Christ – is possible.

Elisabeth Moltmann goes into another similar event.[7] She points out that in the tradition of the Church according to Luke's account (10:38ff), Martha is almost always regarded purely as a housewife, who on the occasion of Jesus' visit to the two sisters, Martha and Mary, failed to do the right thing, i.e. to concentrate on listening to the words of Jesus, instead of carrying out her duties as hostess. The same Martha, however, is actively involved in the story which has been handed down to us of the raising of Lazarus (John 11). She was the sister of Lazarus. She and her sister Mary had begged Jesus to come and heal Lazarus. When he finally came, after Lazarus had already died, Martha went out to meet him, saying, almost as a challenge, that if he had been there Lazarus would not have died. Nevertheless, she begged him to help. In this dialogue revolving around death and resurrection, Jesus speaks the famous words: "I am the Resurrection and the Life. Whoever believes in me will live, even if he dies, and whoever lives and believes in me will not die eternally. Do you believe this?" Martha answers this, and these are her exact words: "Yes, Lord, I believe that you are the Christ, the Son of God, who is coming into the world." That sounds almost exactly like the famous confession of Peter in Matthew 16, which, at least in the Roman Catholic Church, is the verse on which the Church is founded. The confession of a man, the confession of a woman.... The one founded a Church, the other is overlooked.

---

7. Elisabeth Moltmann-Wendel, *Ein eigener Mensch werden: Frauen um Jesus* (Siebenstern: GTB, 1966).

In both these Biblical examples one can certainly cite much that relativizes or qualifies my observations. Above all, in the second example one can point to Jesus' reaction to Peter's confession, which is indeed lacking in this form in John's Gospel. One can also say of the 1 Corinthians text that it is not certain who really encountered the Risen Christ. There are as many critical debates about the reports of the Evangelists as there are about the Pauline text. I believe, however, that the fact that men have done this with great care throughout the whole history of theology and the Church, has further increased the invisibility of women. It is not my concern at all to prove in detail how great a significance these women have had. I am concerned to make the simple observation that the same mechanisms which between 1983 and 1985 brought about the "silencing" of an ecumenical study were already at work in New Testament times, and that must give us cause for thought. There were apparently patterns of selection which proved themselves to be effective throughout the entire period of patriarchy. Present-day women, both theologians and non-theologians, reject these patterns. They try quite deliberately to rediscover women who have disappeared, to give speech to women who are silent, and they do this in so far as they understand themselves to be subjects and no longer objects of male interpretation and male domination.

One can justifiably raise the question at this point: Why did it take so long for this to happen? I must also ask myself why I overlooked all this for so long. Earlier, for ten years, I too accepted without further question that the central statement of the texts and not the context was the only important thing. We were so profoundly influenced by tradition, which was controlled by men, that for many years many of us did not notice the discrimination at all. Yet apart from saying something about the individual, biographical background, family, religious education, trust in authority, the influence of the proclamation, etc., something must also be said here about the historical context.

Only since the emergence of the women's movement, and by that I mean the "old" as well as the "new" women's movements from the time of the Enlightenment up to the present day, has a new way of thinking become possible in the Church as well as in secular society. Susanne Woodtli, who wrote a good book about "equal rights", said in a paper given in Boldern in 1978 that it was a mistake to maintain that the women's movement goes back to the time of the Enlightenment. She had written that herself in her book, but only because her publisher wanted it, and now she cheerfully recanted this error. The women's movement is as old as patriarchy itself. I would like, however, to confine myself here to the contemporary historical existence of the women's movement, as it was conditioned by the history of ideas, as a historically verified movement, in which women became subjects. This actually began at the time of the Enlightenment and the French Revolution. It is a movement in which women attempted to free themselves inwardly and outwardly from what, according to their growing knowledge, crippled them, mutilated them, prevented them from being themselves, turned them into objects, or into what the claims and indictments on them were and are.

This women's movement took place largely outside the Church, on its fringes, or even in opposition to it. It seems to me that as Christians we must regret this fact. It is an indictment of the claim of the gospel to liberate people, and help people to achieve human dignity, dignity for both men and women of course. According to my understanding of the gospel, the Church should have been in the vanguard of the women's movement, and not bringing up its rear. But this just reveals my dreams of the Church, which unfortunately do not always coincide with reality.

Whatever the historical interrelation may have been, however, much of the force of the gospel has certainly entered into the secular women's movement, but there is also the theological argument that it is precisely in the secularization process that basic elements of the Christian message took shape in worldly form, without its origin being named and without being consciously traced back to this source. If we stick to history, so far as we know it, we can certainly say on this basis that without the women's movement, which has provided a stimulus even within the churches, has spread ideas and contributed substantially to the development of a new self-awareness of women, the point would not have been reached in the churches where women started to ask questions about their own history, of their own accord and in their own way, to reflect on their position in the Church and in theology, and finally to arrive at the discovery that much that they had said and done, much more than they had thought possible themselves, was anticipated and accepted in advance by men. Nowadays women search for their own history and tradition within the Church. Because that is so, and because the women's movement has contributed something essential to it, I should like to recall here one basic principle of the liberation movement, before I go back to theology.

In order to show how close these areas were to one another, let me begin with a few sentences taken from the *Katechismus der Vernunft für edle Frauen* [Catechism for noble women], which the theologian Friedrich Schleiermacher produced about 1800, but which he later unfortunately, under pressure from the Church, withdrew. In this Catechism he produced ten commandments and a confession of faith. The tenth of these commandments is as follows: "Thou shalt covet men's education, art, wisdom and honour." And in the confession of faith, the second sentence runs: "I (woman) believe that I do not live in order to obey or to amuse myself, but to be and to become; and I believe in the power of the will and of education, to bring me ever closer to the Infinite, to release myself from the chains of deformity and to make myself independent of the limits of gender."

These sentences are moulded by the belief of the Enlightenment in the power of reason; it is not for nothing that the word "education" plays a large role in this. Education does not stand here for what we today call "self-fulfilment". It concerns the right of a woman "to be and to become", to liberate herself from what is sharply called deformity, or equally false education. Basically the question was for women to become mature persons. For this they needed the opportunity of education and schooling. So the entry of women to high schools and colleges was a matter of great concern for the old middle-class women's movement, and the outcome of an arduous struggle was that women founded the first colleges for training schoolmistresses and kindergarten teachers, and colleges for social workers, which were in fact previously known as schools for women. These were professions broadly directed at the role of the wife and mother in the family, professions in which, however, social concerns were also involved.

Apart from this movement, started by middle-class women with many different variations, there was another kind of women's movement, a workers' movement. Leonhard Ragaz had already recognized the double approach to women's emancipation in 1911, and expressed it in the following form: "The ladies above and the proletarians below embody then the need of modern woman, which springs from the economic situation. Both are sisters, however little they may want to believe it."

The intellectual roots of the workers' movement lie in Marx, Engels, Bebel, Clara Zetkin, Rosa Luxembourg, and others. From the start the liberation of women was seen here as a question of sharing the liberation of human beings. The most important book was August Bebel's, *Frau und Sozialismus* [Woman and socialism], which appeared in 1879, and had run through 162 reprints by 1973. Bebel emphasized the double oppression of women, i.e. their economic dependence on men and men's access to their bodies. Marriage is seen as an institution providing means of support and the only possibility for socially acceptable sexual activity. As a consequence of this, women are educated to obey. Bebel was outraged by prostitution, and this coincided with the concerns of the middle-class women's movement. He expected the liberation of women to come about through the abolition of the class system. He enthusiastically advocated the new society in which women would have equal rights. Functions which in the past were performed by the family should be taken over by public institutions, so that women could enter fully into the production process. In this way, their economic independence from men would also be guaranteed.

As women became visible through the middle-class movement, as well as through the working-class movement of men and women, so in ways different from those in the past they became a public issue, not always and in every case in the way that they themselves wanted to be. There were also not a few causes of friction with the Church. In studying the women's movement, I have already very frequently found in more recent documentation the inference that the churches opposed these endeavours. On the other hand, it must be said also that in many places, in the so-called mission field as much as in our own countries, there were church circles, and on the Catholic side religious orders, who created the first educational opportunities for young girls. It is therefore not entirely justifiable to speak only of rejection of or opposition to these changes by church circles, although this was considerable. The consequence of this opposition was, and remains to this day, that a large number of the women active in the women's movement lost contact with the Church. Here also one historical text, (but this time from a woman), can stand for many. It comes from a book written by a German woman, Malwida von Meysenburg (1816–1903), *Memoiren einer Ideal- istin* [Memoirs of an Idealist]:

> For the first time I said to myself quite clearly that one must liberate onself from the authority of the family, no matter how painful that might be, as soon as it leads to the death of individuality and the submission of freedom of thought and conscience to a particular form of conviction. The freedom of individual convictions and a life consistent with these is the first of the rights and the first of the duties. Up until now women have been excluded from this sacred right and this equally sacred duty; only the Church and marriage had justified the girl's leaving her place in the family, which nature had given her. In the Catholic Church the virgin is permitted not only to exchange the family for the cloister, but to gain merit for it, and through marriage she leaves the family and follows her husband. But in other areas of human activity, women were forbidden to have any convic- tions and to act on them. I saw then that it was time to remove this prohibition, and I said to myself that I would not be able to respect myself if I did not have the courage to

give up everything in order to justify my conviction through action.

She faced the consequences of her attitude in her own life. She left her family, founded a high school for girls in Hamburg, which however only lasted a short time, emigrated, left the Church, became a follower of Feuerbach, and later a friend of Nietzsche. She died in Rome in 1903. Her memoirs proved an authentic voice for many women and girls, to which they could listen, and in which they could discover something about themselves.

No one can say how much really happened through the changes brought about by the earlier women's movement, which came to a definite end in the 1920s. One thing certain is that economic developments, or industrialization, to reduce it to a simple formula, had a very great effect on the changes that women had to confront. Generally speaking, it is the same today: women, depending on whether they are needed in the economy or not, are either lured out of the house or are confined to it, without their being able to defend themselves successfully against this process. However, the voices of women have contributed to the fact that the equality of men and women has been realized in law to an increasing degree, even if often not in actual fact. That is something which has not only been taken seriously even in the churches, but which has also led to definite results.

At this point we must refer to the often forgotten role of the denominational women's organizations, which, of course hesitatingly, but still to an increasing degree, took up the concerns of the secular women's movements. On the basis of my own research and recollections, I venture the opinion that in the period between the earlier women's movement and the modern movement, it was precisely the denominational and ecumenical women's organizations within the churches that took up the concerns of the secular women's movement in their own way, and conveyed them to a large number of women who were not included in the original women's movement, or hardly so. Specifically, I am thinking of the years between the end of the second World War and 1968/70, or even later. During this period much work was undertaken in small and large groups in many Protestant and Catholic organizations, something which was established by the earlier women's movement. From my own past, I remember very well that for many years I resisted understanding or using the word "emancipation" positively. Of course I was actually an "emancipated" woman, but I did not like the word. As a Christian, I had the impression it implied something resistant to God's order. I have found the expression "emancipation run wild" in something I wrote. At the same time, however, I kept countless articles about the task of Protestant, or rather Christian, women in the present age, about the Christian woman's conflict with the changing world, etc. Obviously, I was not the only one who did that. I am thinking of, in the Catholic world for example, the books of Elisabeth Gössmann and Elisabeth Schüssler Fiorenza, which first appeared in the early 1960s. I am also thinking of a series of lectures which the Basel theologian Dorothee Hoch published in 1959, under the title *Weg und Aufgabe der Frau heute* [The way and task of woman today], and of Charlotte von Kirschbaum's book *Die wirkliche Frau* [The real woman], which appeared in 1949. In the Christian sphere, women were beginning to reflect on their own path, in a debate with the ideas of the secular women's movement.The World Council of Churches had already at its inaugural World Assembly, held in Amsterdam in 1948, set up a commission on the "Life and Task of Women in the Church", and instituted a great enquiry among its member churches about what roles and functions women had in the churches. The results of this enquiry were published by a woman, Kathleen Bliss.

This development was very significant. It let women's voices be heard, and showed the restrictions under which women find a voice in the churches of the world. It was an act of great progress that the World Council of Churches then not only founded a commission, but appointed a distinguished woman to further these concerns. This was a Frenchwoman, Madeleine Barot, of the Reformed Church. Many consultations between women and men were planned and executed from her office. It was also she who, on the fringes of the Second

Vatican Council, brought together women from the member churches of the WCC and the women who were eventually allowed to take part as "auditrices", and it was she who seized the initiative to set up a meeting and a working party of Roman Catholic women and women from the WCC member churches at the highest level. So the voices of women became audible; the only question is: who really listened to them and took them seriously?

Because younger women had the impression that they were indeed not heard and were not taken seriously, the second wave of the women's movement broke in the 1960s in the USA, and, with a change of emphasis, in Europe. If the first women's movement had achieved equality within an un-changed system, women after 1968 were concerned with the liberation of the whole of humanity, and with a profound change in society. The oft-quoted saying of Dorothee Sölle, that it could no longer be a question of a fair share of the existing cakes, but of baking new cakes, shows something of the significance and spirit of this movement.

Another text from the same author makes the point even more clearly:

> We do not want
> to become like men
> in our society
> crippled beings
> under pressure to achieve
> emotionally impoverished
> made into bureaucratic objects
> pushed into specialization
> condemned to make a career ...
>
> We do not want
> to learn what men can
> to dominate and to command
> to be served and to conquer
> to hunt to exploit to subdue.[8]

---

8. Dorothee Sölle, *Die revolutionäre Geduld* (Berlin: Fietkau, 1974).

Two things lie behind these very forceful words: the strong self-awareness of a woman, and a radical critique of a one-sided world, dominated by men.

This strong self-awareness has grown in opposition, as women noticed that, after a long struggle to achieve their rights, they had still not attained their goal of liberation. With the upswing of the economy, and after certain successes of the earlier women's movement, the new slogan was "partnership", doing everything together. The hour of the women's movement is past, the hour of partnership has dawned! Many women, however, noticed that they were coming up against new internal and external barriers. They realized that they no longer had to prove that they were just as "good" as men, that the masculine way of speaking and of taking decisions had no relevance to them. They recognized that they wanted to do something quite different. They wanted to be allowed to be and to become themselves, that is, they wanted to reclaim for themselves, too, the values ascribed to them in society, which were always relegated to second place and labelled as feminine, such as empathy, sensitivity to the needs of others, caring, patience, tenderness, service, and to fill them with meaning.

They were told that these characteristics or virtues were inborn, given by nature, biologically based. Now they realized that these "virtues" had been learned and adopted in a situation of bondage and oppression, within a social and ecclesiastical framework to which they had neither consented nor contributed. They wanted, rather, to practise those "virtues" which are labelled as masculine, such as being intellectual (ultimately, they wanted to be allowed to be as bright as they were), having a will of their own, initiative, energy and the ability to get things done, courage. In Sölle's book these appear to be just as perverted as the feminine virtues, if they are restricted exclusively to private life. The so-called masculine virtues are perverted in our world by the economic, political, military and ecclesiastical structures created by men. The women in the new women's movement did not want, and do not want, to take on either the manly delusion of over-estimating one's importancee or the womanly delusion of under-estimating oneself out of humility. Instead, many of them wanted, and want to be, as women, whole people without fixed characteristics and roles, and many of us dreamed and dream of a world in which women and men together can fashion public and private life. Yet there exists an important difference between the constraint and bondage of women and that of men: women's lack of freedom is forced upon them by structures shaped by men. This also applies when women have accommodated themselves so much that they benefit from the system. It is indeed much more comfortable to play second fiddle, to keep in the background, but also to be, in a certain sense, protected. Men's lack of freedom, however, is based on masculine power in public life, certainly not on the power of all men. The exercise of power and violence over men by men, as well as over sons, employees, servants, and men of other classes and races, really does exist. But men on the lowest rung of society still have one or several women "under" them. Because the chances of men relinquishing power for the present – with certain exceptions – are very small, a separate women's culture has come into existence: women's groups, in which women have opened their hearts to each other, exchanged experiences, mutually strengthened each other, and helped each other toward self-awareness: women's banks: women's bookshops: women's music: women's bands: women's conferences, from which men are excluded. There is also new thinking about violence against women, which has led to hostels for battered wives, to action on behalf of exploited women from the Third World (sex tourism), to the struggle for the liberation of abortion laws, in the sense of full responsibility, or at least co-responsibility, of those most affected.

This second wave of the women's movement has made women visible and audible, often in ways which many women and men could not follow. It meets with resistance, and therefore often withdraws into itself. In the churches it has met mainly with disapproval, with the result that, on the one hand, many women in the Church turn their back on it, and, on the other, that the Church generally has a "bad Press" in the movement, and is seen only as an instrument of oppression.

How women within the Church confront their own tradition and their new identity as women will be the subject of the following chapter. I should like to close this chapter with a quotation from a WCC publication. In 1971 it devoted an issue of the formerly monthly journal *Risk* to the theme of the women's movement, with the provocative title "Gladly we rebel". In an article by a woman about women's liberation and the Church, it says:

> Since the first century, the Church has been one of the chief oppressors of women by virtue of its hand-in-hand relationship with the world. While the Gospel affirms that Christians have a responsibility to stand over against the world when it posits its values as ultimate, yet the Church has continually perpetuated the very social institutions, customs and myths which it is called to criticize. With regard to the lives of women, the Church has given rise and support to the myths of dependency and emotionality, the nuclear family system, the all-male Trinity. The values implied in these and other areas have worked to reinforce the cultural patterns which prevent women from living fulfilled lives. Thus the implications of the women's liberation movement for the Church are both manifold and thoroughgoing.

It is precisely in the rebellion against conformity to the cultural norm that women have begun to be most articulate about their hopes, ideals and goals for the future. While the movement may appear to the casual observer as having a purely negative thrust, in fact its orientation is constructive and full of hope.[9]

---

9. Davida Foy Crabtree, "Women's Liberation and the Church," *Risk* Vol. 7, no. 1 (1971).

Chapter 2

Women, Bible, Tradition

IN THE first chapter we familiarized ourselves with the phenomenon of the invisibility of women in the Church, and then saw how women first became visible and audible in so-called secular organizations, and how that was hesitatingly accepted in the churches. Now I should like to turn to a subject which we have already touched upon, but which deserves further treatment, namely the question of how women approach the Bible, and how in turn the Bible is used in the argument with women.

Within the part of the women's movement that still has contact with a church and still consciously seeks to call on the Christian tradition and refer back to it, the Bible naturally still plays a decisive role. Women, both theologians and non-theologians, began to read the Bible with their own eyes a long time ago and to relate it with growing consciousness to their own experiences. There are two sources of motivation for this:

1. Very many women have a strong personal relationship to the Church and its foundation, and they have lived, consciously or unconsciously, by the liberating powers of the gospel. As a result of their growing self-awareness in the women's movement, they have set about investigating these liberating powers independently. In this way they have made their own discoveries, and they have often opened up a new approach to the Bible, involving sometimes painful experiences.

2. For women, Christians and post-Christians alike, part of these painful experiences was seeing that certain biblical texts were continually used against them. They must have experienced the Bible being used as a weapon, not only in the hands of men, both theologians and non-theologians, but also by conservative and anxious women. I remember very vividly,

for example, the fight for women's suffrage. How many times did we women have it said to us that "the woman must be silent in the congregation" (mis-quotation of 1 Cor. 15:34). This biblical text was frequently used by men who otherwise had no recourse to the Bible, who nevertheless used even this weapon in the struggle against the rights of women. Other similar texts were those about the subordination of women (Eph. 5:22ff), or the picture of woman drawn in 1 Peter 3: the quiet, withdrawn, modest, domesticated woman. These texts were used as a weapon against women's demands for their rights, against the emancipation of women. They led to a counter-movement, but also to the very painful discovery that it was not only a question of misunderstanding and false inferences from biblical texts in these cases. The majority of us argued in this way several decades ago. Today we recognize more and more clearly something that I will formulate as a question: Is this just a matter of confused vision, or is it not much more a question of the massive justification of claims to power? Claims to power by a church, claims to power by its office-bearers, claims to power by an academic theology? A feminist exposition of the Bible must ask these questions. We shall come back to that later.

Here I should like to insert a relatively old story of women's experience with the Bible. At the end of the last century there was already a "Woman's Bible" in the USA. It arose out of precisely the experience I have described: women were confronted with the fact that certain biblical passges were always being used against them. Therefore some women decided to publish in a new form the parts of the Bible, in both Old and New Testaments, which dealt with women *"expressis verbis"*, and to provide a commentary. A well-known feminist, Elisabeth Cady Stanton, who had done great service for the emancipation of women, was behind this undertaking. A team of women, which also included a few non-Americans, applied themselves to the work, and edited this "Woman's Bible", which contained commentary on passages from Genesis, the rest of the Pentateuch, the Book of Judges, 1 and 2 Kings, 1 and 2 Chronicles, the Prophets, the Epistles, and Revelation. The women who undertook this exercise were not unbelievers.

They were not heretics, but women who were very concerned
not to cede the Bible to their opponents. They sought instead
to re-interpret the passages which in their opinion did them an
injustice. How clearly they recognized the situation in those
days may be illustrated by a quotation from Elisabeth Cady
Stanton's introduction to this strange edition of the Bible.
There she says:

> These familiar texts are quoted by clergymen in their
> pulpits, by statesmen in the halls of legislation, by lawyers
> in the courts, and are echoed by the press of all civilized
> nations, and accepted by woman herself as the "Word of
> God". So perverted is the religious element in her nature,
> that with faith and works she is the chief support of the
> church and clergy: the very powers that make her eman-
> cipation impossible. When, in the early part of the nine-
> teenth century, women began to protest against their civil
> and political degradation, they were referred to the Bible for
> an answer. When they protested against their unequal
> position in the church, they were referred to the Bible for an
> answer. This led to a general and critical study of the
> Scriptures.[1]

Elisabeth Cady Stanton describes then how she came to edit
her "Woman's Bible" with a committee of women. The fate of
this book is of interest now. It was violently rejected by the
National American Woman Suffrage Association, which she
had founded with other women. Behind this lay the fear that
this book which, so to speak, affected the foundations of
church and state, could harm the cause of women. The women
did not want to pick a fight with the seats of power in church
and state. This is why they condemned this book, which really
should have aided them. So it disappeared from the scene, but
it was handed down in families from mother to daughter, or
from aunt to niece. So it survived, and in 1974 it was reprinted
and published by a women's group in Seattle. In the editors'
foreword to this edition the story is told of how this book came

---

1. *The Woman's Bible* (New York: European Publishing Co., 1895. Facsimile
reprint Edinburgh: Polygon Books, 1985), Part 1, p.8.

into the hands of a woman who had contacts with the new women's movement. In this way it was preserved for us and re-issued. Obviously we today cannot so easily appropriate these interpretations, but I think this story important, because it shows on the one hand how early on it was that committed women became involved in a debate with the Bible, but also how difficult this path was, and is, even today. A slice of the history of oppression and a slice of the joy at re-discovery belong together just as indissolubly now as then, a hundred years ago. This is not a phenomenon of the last fifteen to twenty years, but goes back much further, and it obviously has something to do with the fact that we live in a patriarchal world and an equally patriarchal church.

In Europe too two threads are continually intertwined. Many of us have expended a considerable part of our lives and work in the attempt to prove that – to put it in absolutely direct and straightforward terms – expositions of biblical texts hostile to women do not correspond to the real intention of the texts. I recently looked out a 1958 Swiss list of speakers in a debate with opponents of women's suffrage. A very small part of this brochure, which was conceived as an aid to men and women giving papers in favour of women's right to vote, confronts the same oft-quoted bible texts. The first is that already quoted from 1 Corinthians 14:34, rendered here as: "The woman should be silent in the congregation". It was deliberately quoted from the Vulgate (the Latin translation), which is a falsification of the original Greek, which reads, "Let your wives be silent in the congregations." At this point it says in the brochure:

> In all the admonitions of Paul and the other Apostles, one should not forget that they are set in a particular context and that very particular relationships are presupposed. The fourteenth chapter of 1 Corinthians, from which this verse is taken, deals with the order of worship as a whole. The advice of the Apostle relates to this: women should not disturb the set order with impromptu speech.
>
> The presumed relationships: the women addressed were married women. In the original context, it is not a matter of

an absolute, generally valid abstract command (the woman taken as the representative of all women), but as a very specific command: "Let your wives be silent . . ."

The passage so often quoted and torn out of context does not establish a divine order valid for all times and situations, but gives a directive which is limited to a specific situation, which we cannot broaden out now as we like, without changing the meaning.[2]

When I read this passage (which I actually edited myself) today I conclude:

1. A certain knowledge of historical criticism in biblical exegesis lies behind it. This does not go very far. If one reads contemporary commentaries, one can find the question being raised as to whether this text is by Paul at all, whether it was not inserted during a later controversy, and so on. I do not want to go into this question, but even then one thing was firmly established in the editor's mind: that biblical texts may be and must be interpreted in the light of their own "*Sitz im Leben*". The situation in Corinth is taken seriously. It is established that it deals with a situation which ultimately is not comparable: namely, for the order of worship, a distinction is made in the text concerning the situation of married women who, as it says in the text, could question their husbands at home (or should be able to). All that is a special feature of the text and does not apply to the contemporary situation.

2. It seems to me important to recognize something else today. In the "correction" of this exegesis, it is accepted and goes without saying that, through such a correction or re-interpretation, people who used these biblical texts as weapons could be convinced or could change their opinion. Faith in the power of correct interpretation lies behind this exegesis, as behind many others. Recently I have been variously examining texts and biblical interpretations from the 1950s and 1960s. I always come up against the fact that we attempted to say that

---

2. *In Sinne der Gerechtigkeit und der Demokratie . . . Referentenführer zur Frage der Einführung des Frauenstimm und Wahlrechts in Eidgenässischen Angelegenheiten* (Berne: Arbeitsgemeinschaft der Frauenverbüde, 1958).

the texts were really meant differently from the way in which our opponents expounded them. This statement was doubtless right, at least in the main, even if it was obviously shaped by our own interest, but it did not go far enough or deep enough. We went back to the sources in as far as they were accessible to us, and we were of the opinion that this referring back to the "real intention" must also convince others. Undoubtedly that opened the eyes of many women and even men who were sincerely looking for answers from the Bible, and gave them a certain assurance, and I do not want to abandon these interpretations.

Today we are faced with the knowledge that the history of the *effect* of this text is much stronger, or is so strong that it cannot be shaken by a simple reference to the real intention. How otherwise could it be possible that so much academically accepted historical criticism has wrought no change within our churches (not only as regards "women"), that it remained locked up in the ivory towers of research, which are ultimately not interested in changing the reality of the situation? It has not reached the powers that be, who could bring about changes, nor the "people", who have remained closed to this way of thinking. There are countless good, constructive exegeses of the Old and New Testaments, which open new horizons, but which basically have led to nothing.

If we do not take account in our thinking of what the widespread use of these bible texts has brought about, of what historical effects if has had for women and men, then we will never get any further. It is a matter of recognizing that the history of the effect of some texts is stronger than the explanation of their origin. That applies particularly to what has concerned us here in this chapter: namely, the ignoring of the role of women in the church, the ousting of this role, its misinterpretation, and its suppression.

When I discuss these questions with male colleagues, or talk about some texts, they always counter my arguments with: But it was discovered a long time ago that these interpretations, e.g. of 1 Corinthians 14:34, are wrong. We have known about that for decades. Yes, dear brothers, but why didn't you do anything about it? The history of the effect is part of our common history, even of our common church history. Therefore we must tackle it at a deeper level than the "correct", i.e. right, exegesis of certain texts in the light of historical criticism.

Before giving this further consideration, I should like to draw out another strand of my thesis.

In recent years women have investigated the stories of women in the Bible especially affectionately and intensively. They were looking for their own identity, for biblical figures with whom they could identify, because of their interest in their common history. At the beginning they were amazed how little was known about these women, how little even we ourselves knew, how minor was the role that these women had played in our religious socialization. I am thinking, for example, of how I never thought about what happened to Miriam in the Old Testament. Basically, she saved the life of her brother Moses, but she was not alone in doing so. There was also Moses' mother, who wanted to save her baby son, and before that, there were the Hebrew midwives who, in an act of civil disobedience to the command of Pharoah to kill them all, saved the Jewish boys. Moses' mother, the midwife who assisted her at the birth, Moses' sister, who watched to see that the child who was placed in the basket would be saved, Pharoah's daughter, who actually saved him: they are a whole band of women who made it possible for Moses to take up the role for which God had intended him. His sister Miriam could hardly have played a more prominent role. Think of the Song of Miriam (Exod. 15:20), the ancient victory song of a woman after the crossing of the Red Sea. Why was this woman forgotten afterwards? What really happened to her? We know only that she was punished more severely for her disobedience to Moses than was Aaron, who had done the same thing (Num. 12:1ff), and that she did not reach the Promised Land, any more than her brother did. But who was she really?

I should like to mention one New Testament woman again. She has already appeared once in the previous chapter. I mean Mary Magdalene, and if I mention her so often, then it is with the secret intention and hope that perhaps one of my readers, male or female, will get down to researching this woman's changing history, in the Gnostic Gospels as well as in the New Testament, up to the legend that she was translated in a miraculous way to southern France (I am thinking of her depiction in one of the churches in Assisi). In my opinion, it would be useful to conduct real research into this, something which I cannot do. Essentially, I can draw support for my remarks from Elisabeth Moltmann.[3] She advances the following thesis (as does Ricci): In Luke 8 it is narrated that Mary from Magdala was healed by Jesus. Seven demons were driven out of her. Moltmann (and Ricci) hold that this Mary is mistakenly fused in tradition with the woman who washed Jesus' feet and who was described as a great sinner. Luke gives an account of her in Chapter 7. What could seven demons driven out of a woman be, in the assumptions of men in a patriarchal church, except the demons of sexuality? What other sin could be laid on a woman as a burden, except seduction and provocative sensuality? So it is very understandable that it is not on the basis of the New Testament and the earliest Church, but from later times, that images of Mary Magdalene, showing her as a sinner, continually appear. In Elisabeth Moltmann's latest book,[4] a very impressive picture can be seen. In it Mary Magdalene is kneeling before a high priest in penitential clothing to receive the last sacrament. These pictures – one thinks for example of the famous picture by Tilmann Riemenschneider, which also shows Mary Magdalene as the great sinner – run parallel to another tradition which depicts Mary Magdalene's encounter with the Risen Christ. Which tradition had more effect in the Church? I do not venture to decide. But it is certain that the Church's way of

---

3. E. Moltmann Wendel, *Ein eigener Mensch werden: Frauen um Jesus* (Siebenstern: GTB, 1966). [This research has since been done by Carla Ricci, in *Maria di Magdala e le molte altre* (Naples: D'Auria, 1991). Eng. trans. *Mary Magdalene and the Many Other Women* (Tunbridge Wells: Burns & Oates; Minneapolis: Fortress Press, forthcoming 1993. ED.]

4. *Idem, A Land flowing with Milk and Honey* (London: SCM Press, 1986). The picture is the Tiefenbronn altar by Lucas Moser, 1431. [There is also a bas-relief in the Vieille Major cathedral of Marseilles, showing Mary Magdalene preaching to the princes of the city, reproduced in Ricci, *op. cit.* ED.]

dealing with the figure and history of this one woman has deep roots. To set her free is one of the greatest concerns of present-day feminist theology.

I am thoroughly aware that I have twice already used an emotive word, which I should have dealt with at greater length. I mean the word "feminism" or "feminist". I do not know how often I batter on open doors when I attempt to include a short definition of what I understand by this concept. I must admit that I do not like the word. I dislike all words that end in "-ism", and I continually find that all these "-isms" come out of the same stable, polemically. Marxism, communism, atheism ... all come from the Devil. Racism, sexism ... these are unnecessary abstract words for actual situations from which we wish to disengage ourselves. I can only repeat once again that I have no love for these words, but I do have to live with language as it has been developed, and with what concerns feminism, so as a contemporary woman I must take this word and what it means seriously.

Feminist theology is not the same as "theology of women". Not every theological statement made by a woman or a woman theologian is therefore automatically feminist. European churches would willingly recognize a theology by women while rejecting feminist theology as Marxist, an American import, radical and dangerous. A theology by and of women, yes; feminist theology, no. So I can no longer avoid saying what is meant by this *"terminus technicus"* that has become an emotive word. Feminism is the feeling of being alive for women who were borne on the second wave of the women's movement, or who were borne along for a while by this wave. It is the expression of a new self-awareness and sense of value on the part of women who are on their way and have broken out of their old roles and systems of domination, and who are in search of themselves. These are women who want to understand themselves, no longer as objects, but as subjects, who are searching for their own history and their own identity, and who no longer simply want to be like men. They have freed themselves from male norms, or they at least try to free themselves from them, to make themselves increasingly aware that being fully human includes both things: values traditionally ascribed to women, such as feeling, the capacity for devotion, spontaneity, sensitivity, eroticism, but also the so-called masculine values, such as the ability to think, to see things in abstract terms, to get things done, rationality, practicality. Women oppose the privatization of the so-called feminine virtues. They want these virtues introduced into the whole of society and the Church, not simply as an extension of an unchanged philosophy and theology dominated by men and shaped by masculine thought, but as part of a new society and Church. Feminism today has a campaigning tone and must have it, and it is this that makes people suspicious of it. It needs this campaigning tone, because we live in a completely undisturbed patriarchal Church and society, still dominated by men, and because our theology is still exclusively moulded by men. This applies in general, not only to contemporary theology and consequently to the whole academic world, but it also applies as far back as the establishment of the canon of the Old and New Testaments.

To return once more to the definition of feminism, I should like to go back to Catharina Halkes for this. She gives the following definition:

Feminists are those women who, after their process of emancipation, realize that they have reached a major turning point, because their feeling of unease toward existing structures is still there just as it was before, and who now make it their task to subject the rights and duties, structures, values and standards previously named to criticism, and to examine them for their validity and humanity. For these women, feminism becomes a personal, sometimes painful, but always liberating process, in which we become aware how strongly and to what extent we have made the prevailing culture our own through upbringing and social conditioning, as well as professional training and education, and have internalized it. If we want to be ourselves and contribute constructively to changing a culture that threatens to get bogged down in its one-sidedness and to get out of control in its technological development, then we must step-by-step free ourselves by our own efforts from our alienation.[5]

Feminist theology is the reflection of Christian women on this process in the light of the gospel. Liberation is understood as part of the liberation or redemption which has come into the world from God through Jesus. Feminist theologians cannot avoid understanding even the writings of the Bible as part of an androcentric culture and theology. Therefore, feminist exegesis must subject biblical texts to a different form of criticism from that which our male "brother theologians" formerly used. It too needs scholarly methods, but it needs them with a feminine perspective, directed toward the liberation of women. We shall examine this in the following section.

After this digression, I should like to return to the basic questions that concern us here; that is, I should like to start afresh and attempt to systematize something: How do women with this background read the Bible? What questions do they ask and what criteria do they use? Their point of departure is their own experience, which always remains present and which is always included, the experience of being silenced and of oppression, but also the experience of liberation. Many women have read the Bible selectively for a long time (as I myself did), have lived by certain texts, and have left the rest on one side. For example, they lived by Galatians 3:28, with its whole "called to freedom" theme, and related this freedom to themselves, to their own situation. Or there is the conversation of Jesus with the Woman of Samaria in John 4,[6] or the apocalyptic pictures of the new city, or the banquet of the nations.

But for those of us who have experienced a broadening and widening of our own consciousness through the women's

---

5. C. Halkes, *Gott hat nicht nur starke Söhne* (Siebenstern: GTB,1971).
6. [On this see Anne Primavesi and Jennifer Henderson, *Our God has No Favourites* (Tunbridge Wells: Burns & Oates; San Jose, Ca.: Resource Publications, 1989), ch. 1. ED.]

movement, this selective reading, which basically suppresses part of the problem, no longer suffices. We must also include the negative part, or, to put it another way: we must also include the collective women's experience of oppression by means of biblical texts; we cannot avoid this any more.

Feminist theology is an experiential theology, but it is not simply, and not only, based on personal, subjective experience. In this it does not stand alone in the wider sphere of contemporary theological thought. Its approach is close to that of liberation theology. In that case, it is the experience of poverty and exploitation, in which Christians say: "By taking the real situation seriously, Christ is encountered anew." From that point onwards they have read and are reading the Bible differently. But here also there is not simply *one* theology of liberation, but different theologies according to the situation – in Latin America, in South Africa, in Korea. There are parallels with women too. Here also there is only one approach among all the common interests.

But do we not distort the bible message if we read it, as it were, through the eyes of our own experience? Have we not learned that we must be completely empty, be or become completely free of ourselves, so that we can really hear the Word of God and let ourselves be changed by it?

The counter-question is: Hasn't what has been handed down to us in the Old and New Testaments also been read through certain eyes, and written in this way? This, however, has not been admitted. Indeed I must go another step further: Was not the choice of the books which were accepted into the canon determined by certain interests? For example, to support a particular form of church and to exclude other possibilities (Gnostic and charismatic aspects). Or to go even farther back, had not the redaction of the texts already been made by men in a patriarchal society? Certainly, these men have honestly included the women, but they saw only a part of the reality. Can we women overlook this? Should we really accept that God was simply on the side of men?

Perhaps these questions go too far. Even I quake occasionally at the consequences, but I see my task here as to give, as well and as honestly as I can, an insight into the radical thinking of Christian women, i.e. of women who contine to understand themselves to be Christians, and who would like to be seen as Christians even by those who cannot follow them (or not yet). In this connection, one point must still be considered: a growing number of women will have nothing more to do with the Bible. They regard it as a hopeless undertaking to find anything in this patriarchal book that can help them to believe and to live. They no longer turn to extra-canonical writings either, but to pre-Christian matriarchal cultures. In contrast to them, however, there is a growing number of women who do not want to give up the struggle for an alternative understanding of the Bible, and not only of the texts that expressly speak of women. Therefore, I should like to share the approaches of two American women scholars.

I begin with the book by the New Testament scholar Elisabeth Schüssler Fiorenza, *In Memory of Her.*[7] She recalls the woman who anointed Jesus before his Passion, and of whom he said: "Wherever the Gospel is preached in the whole world, what she has done will be told in memory of her" (Mark 14:9) – which has simply not happened! At the risk of criminally oversimplifying, I should like to present the fundamental principles of her approach in dealing with texts from the New Testament.

She starts out from the basic belief that the redaction, selection and forming of the canon of scripture of biblical texts are all androcentric, i.e. that they were carried out by men in an unreflecting society where patriarchy was taken for granted. According to her conviction, this means that these texts do not hand on the whole reality, or, to put it more precisely, these texts are not the *locus* of revelation. To quote her words: "If the locus of revelation is not the androcentric text, but the life and ministry of Jesus and the movement of men and women called forth by him, then we must develop critical-historical methods for feminist readings of biblical texts."[8]

---

7. E. Schüssler Fiorenza, *In Memory of Her: A Feminist Theological Reconstruction of Christian Origins* (New York: Crossroad; London: SCM Press, 1983).
8. *Ibid.*, p.41.

On the basis of her experience as a woman, she comes to the conclusion that these texts are androcentric; on the basis of her New Testament studies, she comes to the conclusion – incidentally in agreement with renowned male researchers – that the origin of New Testament faith is the Jesus movement, a movement in which women were fully accepted. This reality was concealed by the androcentric transmission, and so we need to read these passages in such a way that "the egalitarianism of the early Christian movement" is brought to light again. This demands a creative critical interpretation: "Such a feminist critical method could be likened to the work of a detective, in so far as it does not rely solely on historical 'facts', nor invent its evidence, but is engaged in an imaginative reconstruction of historical reality."[9]

In order to express what she means by this, she herself quotes another woman theologian, Elizabeth Fox-Genovese, who has written the following: "But to translate silence into meaning requires a critical distance from the tradition as well as immersion in it."[10]

It is clear to Elisabeth Schüssler Fiorenza that the feminist preoccupation with biblical texts cannot be confined to the passages that deal directly with women. To limit oneself to these would already be to appropriate a piece of androcentric redaction, since the passages handed down to us are not central in the biblical message. One would thus be accepting the marginality of women, and furthermore would be engaging in critical dialogue only with women, and not with men and their culture, since they have handed on the whole of the New Testament, and not just these passages. Thus a feminist interpretation of biblical texts is always concerned with the encounter with the whole culture, not only with the authors, but also with the whole tradition which they have handed on, translated and interpreted right up to the present:

---

9. *Ibid.*, pp.35–6.
10. *Ibid.*, p. 42. Quote from E. Fox-Genovese, *USQR* 35 (1979–80). [See also Ricci, *op. cit.*, ch. 1 on the technique required for an "exegesis of silence". ED.]

The systematic androcentrism of Western culture is evident in the fact that nobody questions whether men have been historical subjects and revelatory agents in the church. The historical role of women, and not that of men, is problematic because maleness is the norm, while femaleness constitutes a deviation from this norm.[11]

A feminist analysis of Biblical texts must thus fulfil the following conditions:

1. It must recognize and accept that we have the message only in the form of androcentric texts.

2. From this starting point, it must go back and ask questions about their socio-historical context.

3. It should not only acknowledge contemporary women's experience and their struggle for liberation as the basis of its theology, but must also attempt to reclaim the history of its "fore-sisters", who were both victims and subjects participating in a patriarchal culture. To go back to the basic assumption already quoted: In the Jesus movement and in some congregations of the early Church, which we know only through androcentric texts, women actually had rights and power. To show both and to bring them into the light – the victimization and the strengths of women, which transcend patriarchal limitations – is a basic concern.

4. Like liberation theologians, who deliberately break through the so-called objectivity of academic exegesis, and take the part of the poor, reading the Bible with the eyes of the poor and representing their interests, feminist hermeneutics must take the part of women, and do so in the sense already indicated: the part of those suffering under patriarchy, of those reduced to silence, of the oppressed, and also of the strong and powerful.

5. The aim of this whole book is to win back for women too the stories of faith, which have been told only by men. Our common history should not remain "occupied" by men. It is also women's history, even if it is preserved only in fragments,

---

11. *Ibid.*, p.42.

and women must reconstruct much of it with "creative imagination".

6. The inclusion of extra-canonical scriptures, which play a great role in feminist theology, helps this.

In conclusion, a further quotation from Elisabeth Schüssler Fiorenza:

> In so far as androcentric biblical texts not only reflect their patriarchal cultural environment, but also continue to allow a glimpse of the early Christian movements as a discipleship of equals, the reality of women's engagement and leadership in these movements precedes the androcentric injunctions for women's role and behavior. Women who belonged to a submerged group in antiquity could develop leadership in the emerging Christian movement which, as a discipleship of equals, stood in tension and conflict with the patriarchal ethos of the Greco-Roman world . . . Women had the power and the authority of the Gospel. They were central and leading individuals in the early Christian movement."[12]

Rosemary Radford Ruether presents the relationship between feminism and the Bible in a different way. She is also a professor, a Catholic in a Protestant theological seminary. She adopts certain of Elisabeth Schüssler Fiorenza's positions, but is also criticized by her. There is indeed no single unitary feminist theology, and hopefully there never will be one, for then a process would necessarily stagnate into a system, and that would be a pity. In any case, Ruether is not a specialist exegete, but a systematic theologian, and this determines the difference in their approach.

She also proceeds from the recognition that patriarchy constitutes the social context of the Old and New Testaments, but maintains that both Testaments, and quite independently of the women's question, contain positions which are critical of patriarchy. She discovers these approaches in the prophetic tradition of the Old Testament, and this is taken up by Jesus. She sees in this prophetic, liberating tradition of biblical faith

---

12. *Ibid.*, p.35.

the central tradition of all. As she says: "It chooses a tradition that can be fairly claimed, on the basis of generally accepted biblical scholarship, to be the central tradition, the tradition by which biblical faith constantly criticizes and renews itself and its own vision."[13]

Whether this really is a question of "generally accepted biblical scholarship", I cannot say. I think she should rather stick to the idea that this undoubtedly very strong line of the biblical message fits in with and accords with women's experience. Be that as it may, what interests us more is the existence of this choice and what it leads to.

Ruether makes this prophetic, liberating line into a norm of her biblical reflection on feminism. She first of all comes to grips with certain factors of this tradition/strand. She sees four such elements:

1. God's defence and vindication of the oppressed;
2. The critique of the dominant systems of power and their power holders;
3. The vision of a new age that is to come, in which the present system of injustice is overcome and God's intended reign of peace and justice is installed in history;
4. The critique of ideology, or of religion. Prophetic faith denounces religious ideologies and systems which function to justify and sanctify the dominant, unjust social order.[14]

There is nothing new in all this, nor does Ruether claim that there is. She illustrates these elements in a series of bible passages, and shows how Jesus takes up this tradition in his challenge to the Temple cult and in his confrontations with the scribes and Pharisees, and in the famous passage of Luke 4:18: "The Spirit of the Lord is upon me, because he has anointed me to preach good news to the poor. He has sent me to proclaim release to the captives, the recovering of sight to the blind; to set at liberty those who are oppressed."

---

13. R. Radford Ruether, *Sexism and God-talk: Towards a Feminist Theology* (Boston: Beacon Press; London: SCM Press, 1983), p.24.
14. *Ibid.*

As I said, there is nothing new in all this; it forms the basis of faith of many Christians, men and women of every age. But what is new is the manner in which this biblical line of thought is taken over by feminism, by a feminist woman theologian. It is not only that women are simply lined up in the row of the many oppressed groups on earth – although that is also true. But that is not the main point. Rather, patriarchy itself, the dominant culture in which these texts were formulated, is subjected to this critique. In Rosemary Radford Ruether's own words:

> Feminism appropriates the prophetic principles in ways the biblical writers for the most part do not appropriate them, namely to criticize this unexamined patriarchal framework. Feminist theology that draws on biblical principles is possible only if the prophetic principles, more fully under-stood, imply a rejection of every elevation of one social group against others as image and agent of God, every use of God to justify social domination and subjugation. Patriarchy itself must fall under the biblical denunciation of idolatry and blasphemy, the idolizing of the male as representative of divinity. It is idolatrous to make males more "like God" than females.[15]

She goes on to say that a norm for evaluating and criticizing biblical texts arises from this prophetic critique of patriarchy. Carrying out such evaluations is not new and occurs not only in feminist theology. Even groups which incline toward fundamentalism do not consider all biblical texts to be equally authoritative and equally central, i.e. close to the centre of biblical faith. The only thing that is new is that women, who were always an oppressed group themselves, reduced to silence, and who still are, introduce themselves and their own liberation as an essential criterion, and apply the prophetic critique to patriarchy.

The second element she names seems especially im-portant to women: the critique of the dominant power system.

---

15. *Ibid.*, p.23.

This critique is at the centre of Jesus' message (cf. Mark 10:42 and parallel verses). His words that the last shall be first, or his taking sides with those on the fringes of society, prove this. God takes the side of the oppressed, but Ruether quite rightly says: God does not justify the thirst for vengeance by the oppressed. It is not a question of a crude reversal of the relationships of power, so that the positions are simply changed, but of a very radical transformation: "A revolutionary transformative process that will bring all to a mode of relationship."[16] That applies also to women!

Ruether's idea seems important to me also in that this use of the prophetic tradition by feminism – and this use should never be exclusive, otherwise women lay themselves open to the same criticism as patriarchy –, that this application of the prophetic critique to patriarchy goes beyond the letter of the prophetic message. "Feminist theology makes explicit what was overlooked in male advocacy of the poor and the oppressed: that liberation must start with the oppressed of the oppressed, namely women of the oppressed."[17]

This expansion of the biblical message, as Ruether calls it, says something about her understanding of this message. She does not see these texts as a norm fixed for ever, but as a living message, constantly undergoing a process of appropriation and rejection: "We appropriate the past, not to remain in its limits, but to point to new futures."[18]

These new futures do not, however, arise from fantasies in an airtight vacuum of a tradition-less abstraction, nor from present-day experience, but from the dialogue between the contemporary experience of faith and life and that recorded in biblical texts. It is perhaps a dangerous path, but in my opinion it is a path full of the promise of a new life.

---

16. *Ibid.*, p.30.
17. *Ibid.*, p.32.
18. *Ibid.*, p.33.

Chapter 3

Images Of God – Women's Experiences Of God

As THE etymology of the word shows, "theology" has to do with thinking about God. Women today, both theologians and non-theologians, think a great deal about God inside the Church and outside it. This thinking has led to debates and also to mockery on the part of men. In 1980, when I returned from a study holiday in California, where I had occupied myself with intensive work on the women's movement and feminist theology, a colleague asked: "What have you come up with now? Is God a man or a woman?" I still remember being very hurt by this question. Yet it made me think about the image of God, that is, about questions as to the ultimate meaning of our lives, on the level of normal wisecracks between men and women. Here I hope to succeed in dealing on another level with the most delicate, or one of the most delicate, questions in this context, namely, that of the experience of women with God and with the images of God in the Judaeo-Christian tradition, in a way which does not lead to this kind of suppression of a theme that concerns us all.

I should like to relate my own experience, and then go on to provide an insight into the experiences, thoughts, and theological approaches of other women, as I have done already in the previous chapter. During this study holiday in California we attended the service one Sunday morning in a large Presbyterian church. This church had a famous preacher; the church was full, as it was every Sunday. So the minister was apparently successful. On that particular Sunday he used an image in his sermon – and a very good image it was. He spoke of the world-famous bridge at the entrance to San Francisco Bay, the Golden Gate Bridge. This is familiar to most people, at least from pictures, with its two high pillars or towers and the span sweeping over the bay. The preacher, however, was basically not talking about the bridge, but about the two pillars. These are certainly impressive, and without them there would be no bridge. He explained how these two pillars stand there, indispensable, and he used them as an illustration of the two basic commandments of God: "Thou shalt love the Lord thy God" and "Thou shalt love thy neighbour as thyself". These are certainly basic statements of our Judaeo-Christian faith. These two basic pillars of our faith, he said, have been driven into our history by God "so to speak", as the pillars of the bridge have been driven into the banks of the bay. Nothing is too much for them, they are fixed, and no one could undermine them. They form an unshakable frontier – but against whom, or what? Is God really one who sets limits? During the sermon, in which he described the steadfastness and indispensability of these two commandments, I could hardly sit still and listen. Luckily for me, a piece of paper and a pencil were stuck in the back of the pew in front of me. I seized them and began to draw, although I can hardly draw at all. I drew the two pillars and the span of the bridge, and then closed my eyes and saw in front of me the view of the bridge I could see every day from our flat, and which I often observed at sunset, the bridge whose sweep and colours I loved. I saw in front of me the sun and the sky, I drew the waves and the clouds, and I wrote underneath: "Nothing is too much for them, right. But the bridge exists only with the sun and the water. And the pillars have been built only to enable people to cross over. The pillars are not the world. Neither are they limits to the secret of life. Heaven is higher and the sea is deeper than the towers people have built." And under that I wrote: "Jesus has certainly not been speaking through the words of this man."

He, who was trying to explain something basic with what was really a well-chosen image, clearly gave no thought to the question of why a bridge is built, and he did not see the bridge while he was speaking. He had no feeling for the communication that it creates, or the beauty that is produced by the span arching from one bank to the other. Naturally, I agreed that it needs these two pillars. I would also not dispute the idea that they can be used as an image of the two basic commandments of God, which I regard as important, and of course I know that no illustration can say everything. I can no longer, however, and really I never could, understand God as one who sets immovable boundaries, but only as one who creates life and makes communication possible, and will do so, and as one for whom laws and states of order are flexible measures. It is more important to me that the bridge is crossed, that it serves as a link between two banks separated from each other, than that it hangs from two pillars. They are, admittedly, an indispensable part of the whole, but on their own they are useless. To put it plainly, I can no longer accept a fixed doctrine about God, I no longer believe in a once-for-all exclusive revelation, which we alone can still interpret. No, God is greater; God is also within me.

To put it another way, and to go back to the illustration, God is also in the beauty, in the colours, and in the depths of life – by which I mean the sea. God's commandments are not abstract. God is present and near as the living God, or, in other words, life-force and being-force, mysterious and never completely within our comprehension. Naturally I know that these two sides, spoken and unspoken, were always present in the history of the Church, that this is nothing fundamentally new. But this is not the side that came to carry authoritative weight. It is not the side by which my Church lives. It is the side of enthusiasts or fanatics, those who cross frontiers, heretics, the unreliable; of women, of those who cannot so precisely separate things out, or want to, who do not primarily impose restrictions. Today women, because of what I have described in the previous chapter as a new sense of value and of life, dare to speak of their own experiences with God, and many of us, including myself, have the feeling that we have for a long time been deprived of something through the way in which God is spoken of and taught in men's churches. Many women have the feeling that they have been cheated of something essential, that they have been deprived of access to the source, to the meaning of life, to God. I know that to a considerable degree men also, "laymen", have the same feeling. However, I should like to limit myself here to the statements of women.

Since in feminist theology, as well as the "I", the "we" is an important dimension, in the sense of a shared experience within smaller and larger women's communities, within the "woman church", which naturally is not the whole church, but which for many of us is a piece of our essential spiritual homeland, I should like to relate briefly in what follows how a young woman describes her feminist conversion. She is (once again) an American, and I am drawing on her unpublished thesis, submitted for a master's degree at Berkeley. Her experience seems important to me as a prelude to understanding what I want to say more systematically afterwards about women's experiences and images of God.

This young woman – let us call her Ann – uses the word "conversion" quite deliberately for her personal spiritual path. She says honestly that through her encounter with the women's movement, which gave her a new sense of life and self-esteem, she began to question her own understanding of God and her faith. She knew that for her, real religious experience had been suppressed. She expresses it this way: the experience of a living, life-giving God is translated into expressions that do not question male oppression. God is called Father, and the translation of the experience of a living presence into the image of the Father becomes just as sacred as, or even more sacred than, the original experience. One could put it like this: the formulation, the setting-down of the experience becomes more important than the experience itself. Her questions have grown out of her own life, from her own encounter with love and death, and she suddenly had the experience that, as she puts it, her eyes were opened. At another point in this story she says: "When the world cracks open" – that is, as a curtain is torn. She is driven to anger in this process – I would say to holy wrath – at the perversion of her own innermost, deepest experiences in a sterile patriarchal system. She describes patriarchy as sin. Therefore, conversion, which in Christian language means turning from a state of sin, is the right word for her journey. Feminist conversion, she says, includes the death of our assent to patriarchy, so that we are born anew. This death is also the death of an image of ourselves, and is the death of the image of God as God the Father of patriarchy. Anyone who thinks this path is easy must permit my informant to tell them that the destruction of these images of ourselves and of God by many women is described even by Mary Daly, among others, as experience of nothingness. Because that is so shocking, we fall back on the trusted language of the patriarchal church. This way into nothingness, of no longer knowing, is however, Ann says, grounded in faith. It is the faith that there is a self that can overcome patriarchal roles and identities, it is a faith in meaning that will appear from the chaos of meaninglessness. It is a deeper faith in the reliability of life, but it is clear that this way is contrary to our culture and all church faith, and that it is exceptionally hard to hold on to it.

Anyone who describes questioning, critical women simply as foolish daredevils who play with the most sacred things, does not know what he or she is saying. It could indeed be that God appears on this way through the wilderness, that God has a new name, new names. The gift and the power to name the world has been taken away from women by men. In Genesis 2, Adam is given the right and the opportunity to give names to all living things. Today, women claim this right back, and it is more than a civic right: it is a profound human right to be allowed to give names to the world and even to God.

The passage I have in front of me reads: "The time spent in the wilderness is a time of hope, since we indeed believe in the God who is full of new opportunities. However, we are looking for a new language for our vision, and women have found a new language, their own language, when anybody listens to them." The author of these lines counts herself among those who have experienced in the Christian tradition not only oppression, but also liberation, and she tries to put up with the tension this produces. Other women have chosen a different way. However, to continue in another style, I shall now attempt to present some of the questions women ask about our Church's image of God.

This image is clearly moulded by men, even though this fact is often disputed by theologians. The Persons of the Trinity confessed in the creeds of many churches are all masculine: God the Father, Son and Holy Spirit. The language in services and liturgies is clear: God is the Lord, the King, the Lord of Hosts; one speaks of his action, his Kingdom, to say nothing of hymns such as "Onward, Christian soldiers, marching as to war". Moreover, the history of art speaks a clear message. In often fantastically beautiful pictures painters have transgressed the Old Testament commandment against making images in many ways, and have generally depicted God in the form of a very old man, and Christ, correctly of course, as a young man, although there are many pictures of him that depict him as an almost androgynous youth. The case of the Holy Spirit is more difficult – the dove is a female symbol, the flames are sexually neutral. In any case, however, God the Father is paramount, and ecclesiastical language, in talking of God, always uses masculine articles and pronouns. All this speaks louder than the assurance, continually heard and quite honestly intended, and verifiable in many ways, that God is obviously not exclusively one sex or the other. Men who are not aware of themselves and of their own position within the Church, and who accept this without question as God-given, are not wounded by this, and can easily dismiss women's criticism as laughable and trivial.

How then do women cope with their growing unease, their anger, with starting to see and hear?

Many of us have begun to look for texts in the Bible in which God's feminine side finds expression, directly or indirectly. I am thinking, for example of Isaiah 66:13, where it is said of God: "As one whom his mother comforts, so I will comfort you," or Psalm 84 where the altars of God are described: "My heart and flesh sing for joy to the living God. Even the sparrow finds a home, and the swallow a nest for herself, where she may lay her young, at thy altars," and then to my disappointment it continues, "O Lord of hosts, my King and my God." At any rate it is clear in this Psalm that there is a deep sense of security in being with God, which we rightly or wrongly associate with Mother, and this is expressed in the metaphor frequently found in the Psalms: that we find rest "under the shadow of thy wings". In an ecumenical creed drawn up by women it is put: "I believe in the Holy Spirit (or the Holy Spiritess), the female Spirit of God, who created us like a hen and brought us into the world and covers us with her wings." Jesus' dealings with women also belong, of course, to this series of discoveries, but not them alone: so does the special idiom he uses to talk about God. I am thinking of the well-known parables in Luke 13, where he first of all talks of the Kingdom of God using the image of a grain of mustard seed which someone (presumably a man) sowed in his garden, then as leaven, which a woman took and hid in her dough. In Luke 15 it is a shepherd looking for a lost sheep, and a woman looking for a lost coin until she has found it. Jesus addressed the Father with a very intimate form of the word for father, but in our church tradition it has been handed down as: "I believe in God, the Father, the Almighty. . . ." This Father then became increasingly the head of the patriarchal order. His features have continually become sterner, and the picture of the father who went out to meet his son returning from a far country to enfold him in his arms has become fainter and fainter – and not only for women.

In many places women have fought for God to be addressed as "our Father and our Mother". This is something I have experienced in many church services. There are also many attempts not to continue simply with "he" but to say or write "he or she", when speaking of God. Writing this is easier than saying it. In this connection, it is interesting to note the principle Rosemary Radford Ruether adopts in her book:

> When speaking of the understanding of the divine of the ancient Near East, I speak of Gods and Goddesses, making clear that paired male and female concepts were used. These terms are capitalized, rejecting the traditional Western usage that left them lower-case to signal that these were false deities and not the true (Judaeo-Christian) God. When speaking of the divine within the Judaeo-Christian tradition, I use the term God. This is understood to be a male generic form and thus inadequate to express the vision of the divine sought in this theology. It does not imply, however, that there are not usable and authentic intimations of divinity

found within traditional Jewish and Christian under-
standings of God.

Finally, when discussing the fuller divinity to which this
theology points, I use the term God/ess, a written symbol
intended to combine both the masculine and feminine forms
of the word for the divine while preserving the Judaeo-
Christian affirmation that divinity is one. This term is
unpronounceable and inadequate. It is not intended as
language for worship, where one might prefer a more
evocative term, such as Holy One or Holy Wisdom. Rather
it serves here as an analytic sign to point toward that yet
unnameable understanding of the divine that would transcend patriarchal limitations and signal redemptive experience for women as well as men.[1]

The idea that God can not be only masculine should find
expression in all these ways. In the service book compiled for
the WCC Assembly in Vancouver, there is a form of blessing
that gives expression to the same concern in another way:

The blessing of the God of Sarah and Abraham,
the blessing of the Son who was born of Mary,
the blessing of the Holy Spirit, who watches over us
like a mother over her children, be with us all. Amen.

An American women's song addressed to a little girl – it is
a secular song, but these secular songs contain a great deal of
women's spirituality – ends: "May the warm wind caress you,
may God smile upon you, may she bless you." These entirely
separate but parallel attempts have a two-fold basis. On the
one hand the search for an inclusive image of God that, as
Ruether says in the passage already quoted, "transcends
patriarchal limitations", and on the other hand the struggle for
another, relevant, language. A few word on both points:

Language should not forever exclude us women. It should,
for example, also make one aware of the problem, through
provisional, unsatisfactory formulations such as the clumsy

---

1. R. Radford Ruether, *Sexism and God-talk: Towards a Feminist Theology* (New York: Crossroad; London: SCM Press, 1983), pp.45–6.

"he/she". Attempts should be made to speak inclusively, not exclusively, that is to include and not to exclude women. There are already some women and men ministers in the Protestant churches – and presumably some men ministers in the Catholic Church – who are at least concerned about such language. It is very difficult and very tedious, but I am of the opinion that it is worth the trouble, even if it is only a tiny step on the long journey towards a solution of the real problem. It is already a help to me when I feel that people, women and men, have sat up and taken notice, and have tried to make plain something of what they have understood by the way they speak.

The other point, however, is the tentative effort to get us away from a narrow image of God, narrow because it is fastened down in masculine language and imagery. There is another side to the Bible, and this has led people to attempt to broaden the form of addressing God to "Father and Mother". For many this already goes too far and borders on blasphemy. For myself, I wonder whether it goes far enough, whether it helps me at all. Do I really want to see Mother put alongside Father? Do I want to see parents, as it were, in heaven, possibly adding to pressures to bind me forever to a childish – infantile, even – phase? Does that solve any of my real problems? I respect the attempts to address God as Mother. They draw aside a veil, but I really do not want to remain dependent on heavenly parents. The juxtaposition of Father and Mother, which is of crucial significance for an essential part of the life of every human being, is so strongly stamped by our middle-class ideas of the family in a patriarchal society, that it does not help me very much in finding my identity and so satisfying my deepest yearning for meaning.

There are ways I find more helpful. I should like briefly to note two of these here. In doing so I take up an idea Catharina Halkes expressed in a recent book. In a definition of her position, set out *inter alia* in a controversy with the goddess movement (which I shall come to shortly) she says:

It always moves me to see the relief and joy of numerous women when they discover that God isn't a man at all.

These images are so firmly anchored in our culture and religion ... Naturally it is not a question of the gender of God, as we theologians say, yet it appears that in actual fact people experience the activities ascribed to God as nevertheless masculine or paternal. Therefore I give priority to the transfer, for the present, of the accent on to the immanence of God.[2]

Two expressions are important for me in the last sentence: "immanence", meaning either the immanence of God in the world or in her own experience, her own life, and "for the present". These are definitions "along the way", and they are changeable. Two related passages are important for me personally, one from Mary Daly and the other from Exodus 3. First Mary Daly. In her book *Beyond God the Father*, which appeared as early as 1973, she writes:

Why indeed must "God" be a noun? Why not a verb – the most active and dynamic of all? Hasn't the naming of God as a noun been an act of murdering that dynamic verb? And isn't the verb infinitely more personal than a mere static noun? The anthropomorphic symbols for God may be intended to convey personality, but they fail to convey that God is Be-ing. Women now who are experiencing the shock of non-being and the surge of self-affirmation against this are inclined to perceive transcendence as the verb in which we participate – live, move and have our being.[3]

What is meant here is the power of being or of be-ing, the being which is in the process of becoming – a paraphrase that always conveys sympathy or concern and also includes the approach to creation, to the cosmos. Admittedly, life and wholeness, power and movement are not given content here. For Mary Daly, the sisterhood within the women's movement quite definitely lies behind this process. To put it in my own words, with which she would presumably not agree: "This living being is, in its innermost essence, love."

2. C. Halkes, *Suchen was verlorenging* (Siebenstern: GTB, 1977), pp.100ff.
3. M. Daly, *Beyond God the Father* (Boston: Beacon Press, 1973), p.23.

I turn now to the Bible: Exodus 3:14 deals with the revelation of God to Moses, and with his call to lead the people of Israel out of bondage in Egypt. Moses asks what God's name is, because he must tell his people who the God is who calls them to liberation. God answers his question with a description of himself, which is usually translated as: "I am who I am". This statement has given rise to a mass of clever philosophical discussion. Currently, this runs something like: God did not want to reveal his name, since he is a *deus absconditus*, the hidden God; the intention of the statement is rather to conceal, to show humans their limit. Moses did not need to know anything more than that he had heard the call to lead the Exodus. Now there are, however, completely different interpretations of the Hebrew, since the form of the verb "to be" used here can also be understood as the future. Years ago the translation and interpretation by Hans Heinrich Schmid, Professor of Old Testament studies at the University of Zurich, made a strong impression on me. He suggests this translation, which has stayed in my mind: "I am the one who will reveal myself." The question of who God is, is thus not decided: God will show himself again and again in history. According to biblical understanding, this does not mean that all continuity is thereby destroyed, but that he who now reveals himself as liberator and who calls people to liberation, will always reveal himself as such in the future.

What prevents me from incorporating this explanation in our search and our problems as women? God is the living God; God does not allow himself to be tied down, certainly not to a purely male-fashioned image. I could enlarge on Schmid's translation in a feminist way and say: "I am the One who, male or female, will reveal Myself." This means that this hope goes with us on our women's way through the wilderness, that a new encounter with God can take place, that "his" inconceivable Being in a new situation will make known a new aspect, that liberation can mean not only an Exodus from Egypt, but also an Exodus from patriarchy. This does not mean a breach with the tradition continually handed on to us to guide our steps. It does mean, however, a turning away from the all too hard-and-fast definitions and descriptions of God.

This translation leads us into the open and leaves the question of the gender of God open. In other words, it transcends this question. Given this, I too can concur that it is not God's gender that is the point at issue. Remember the quotation from Catharina Halkes given above. It ends: "In my opinion, there is a way in which we can remain true to the orientation that proceeds from Scripture, from Christ and from tradition, if we only treat it imaginatively and creatively, and place new emphases on it that keep us moving critically forwards."[4]

I should like to add a note to the text from Exodus: It is certainly no coincidence that the description God gives of himself occurs in the story of a call. God's revelation of himself is not an end in itself. Where a human being becomes aware of divine power, power for living and acting, his or her life will be changed, and a charge will be laid upon him or her, or else divine love and presence are revealed in the charge itself. This biblical component, which goes beyond every form of mere introspection or self-awareness or navel-gazing, is for me an indispensable component of my own faith and life.

Having given some indication at the outset of the direction in which my own reflections might proceed, I should like to embark on what is, in my opinion, an important digression, and try to make a brief presentation of the completely different kinds of ways in which contemporary women study and experiment with rituals. I have in mind the phenomenon described by the term "matriarchal spirituality". This starts from the assumption that matriarchal societies existed from the beginning of human culture. From the point of view of us women, these societies must represent our roots. Their existence has been proved by archaeological research into the remnants of cultures. They are also reflected in many myths. One misunderstanding must be cleared up immediately: the women who lovingly investigate this matriarchal culture and hold it up as a helpful Utopia for the future, do not seek to reverse existing relationships, i.e. to give women dominance in much the same way as men (and even women) dominate

---

4. Halkes, *op. cit.*, p.74.

under patriarchy. Their concern is rather – and for me this is the most relevant and convincing thing in these enquiries – for forms of society free of hierarchy. Research is said to have shown that complete co-operation existed between men and women; this was closely connected with the rhythms of nature, and thus protected these. The Munich philosopher Heide Göttner-Abendroth has not only written widely-read books, such as *Die Göttin und ihr Heros* [The Goddess and her Hero],[5] but together with other women has also tried (and is still trying) to devise rituals, rituals that follow the rhythm of the seasons or the phases of the moon. If I have correctly understood the argument, in its essentials it goes as follows: An all-powerful Father God should not be replaced by an equally powerful Mother God, but rather the image of the Goddess is seen in threefold form. Firstly as the young, spring-like maiden who seeks after and catches hold of life; her symbols are bow and arrow and the sickle-shaped new moon, as shown in pictures of Diana, not to mention the common depiction of Mary in which she appears against the back-ground of, or with her feet resting on, a new moon. The second form is the mature woman, who "with her erotic power makes earth and water fruitful, and thereby sustains life". The full moon corresponds to her. In summer she consummates the sacred marriage with the hero. The third form is the old crone. She lives in the underworld; she corresponds to the waning moon; she destroys life – in winter – and at the same time causes it to rise again. "She is the mysterious goddess of the eternal descent and the eternal return; she determines the astronomical cycles (the rising and setting of the stars) and thereby the cycles of plant life and of human life. Thus she is the mistress of the cosmic order, and personifies eternal wisdom." In every stage of his life, man relates to one of these forms. He does not represent the cosmos. In spring his initiation takes place, often, as in fairy tales, through the accomplishment of difficult tasks; in summer there is the festival of the sacred marriage; in winter his death, understood

---

5. H. Göttner Abendroth, *Die Göttin und ihr Heros. Frauen-offensive* (Munich, 1980), pp.17, 20.

as self-sacrifice, "in order to keep the cosmic regions fertile for the following year through his blood". The dominance of the multiform female deity is unambiguous. The symbol of the hero is the sun, which is understood as being dependent on the moon in matriarchal cultures. It changes colour between red and gold, while the moon keeps its own colour and furthermore determines the tides, the growth of plants and the cycles of female fertility. The rituals of contemporary women follow the changing of the seasons, the solstices, the equinoxes, but from the position of the moon.

Many women today feel that such images, myths and rituals speak to them very strongly, they feel their own powers, which had long been suppressed, becoming alive again; they can participate actively. Rather than adopting all these old ideas in detail, these rituals express a fulfilment of life, in which they can take part. When I, by way of comparison, think of the dearth of opportunities for participating in our church services, I can understand something of the attraction in this. Catharina Halkes refers in this connection to an article by Carol Christ, "Why Women need the Goddess".[6] The reasons she gives seem to me an aid to our understanding. First, the recognition of female power and might: "If I feel weak, it is she – a goddess – who can help me and protect me. When I feel strong, she is the symbol of my own power. At other times I experience her as the natural energy in my body and in the world." A second point is: the goddess confirms, so to speak, the life cycle of women, the different seasons of life as well as their bodily cycle. A third is that the goddess stands for the fact that women can also have a will of their own. In patriarchal tradition women have been forced to be always passive, to let things happen, beginning with Mary's, "Be it unto me", and going on with woman's continual waiting, waiting for something to happen, waiting for the man who is active in the "world" to come back to her. The goddess symbolizes the fact that women too can have a will. And finally the strong ties

6. C. Christ, "Why Women need the Goddess", C. Christ and J. Plaskow, eds. *Womanspirit rising: A Feminist Reader in Religion* (San Francisco: Harper & Row, 1979), pp.278–9.

between women, and particularly those between mother and daughter are emphasized, as exemplified by Demeter and Persephone, the mother who had to give her daughter for part of the year to the underworld, as consort of the god of the underworld. Then nature mourns in winter, and is woken to life again when the daughter returns to her mother. This myth makes clear that a bond between mother and daughter can be stronger than that between man and wife.

For us as Christians, male or female, or even as Children of Israel, it is difficult to come to terms with these ideas. The worst thing we can do is simply to dismiss them out of hand and exclude them. We should remember that such a thing has already happened once, but that the history of the Church shows examples of inclusion following exclusion. Each has its own dangers. The patriarchal form of the Church is made increasingly rigid by rigid exclusion, and women are once more branded as witches. Inclusion seems equally impossible to me, even if in the early Church heathen temples and practices were used and re-interpreted, and some of their content has entered into our own history. It is not for nothing that we celebrate Christmas at the winter solstice. And how much of the substance of pre-biblical deities, for example, has seeped into the images and piety of the cult of Mary? Such inclusion would, I think, be unacceptable today. It does not do justice to the exploration of layers of which we know little; it is a quick attempt at a possible solution. I feel we should not let the dialogue be broken off. Catharina Halkes, who has clearly distanced herself from the cult of goddesses, says in the work already quoted:

> For me it is entirely clear and understandable that at a time when women are discovering how much they are con-strained by the dominant system of symbols and therefore also by the underlying reality they express, they should return to the images of an earlier culture and to nature symbols that can be identified with the "feminine" (the moon, to a certain extent, but also the womb). We need this as a reaction to the one-sidedness and dominance under which we have suffered. Naturally the plea for exclusively

feminine symbols contains the danger of another one-sidedness. But I should not consider that a bad thing – as a temporary measure and as an expression of transition. It seems to me to be good shock therapy for those who have still hardly considered the question, and as therapeutic and affirmative for those who already face this problem. However, I do not believe that the solution to this problem is to be found here for those who feel themselves bound to the Jewish-Christian tradition of faith.[7]

This is why I plead for the discussion not to be broken off. We need to listen to what this matriarchal spirituality and these rituals, so closely tied to nature, have to tell us, for the first time or anew, of the frustration and rediscovery of the cosmos, of creation and human nature. We should not be timid just because they introduce a new image of God. We can consider many things without bringing in the *Malleus Maleficarum*. It is still, of course, an open question how far something is now being projected from modern experience back on to much older symbols, themselves human in origin. Indeed this applies to the patriarchal image of God, constructed by men.Only if we are prepared to analize even this, even though – in contrast to matriarchal forms – it has the whole weight of tradition behind it, will we be able to make an equally free and critical analysis of the re-emergent goddesses and their rituals, ancient though they are.

Following the structure of the Christian Trinity, I should now like to come to the second person, Jesus Christ. Can a male Redeemer redeem women? Women are asking this question today. Men, and other women, answer them very quickly: God has become human in the *human being* Jesus Christ. The incarnation of God in the world does not depend on the maleness of Jesus. I believe this too, but to those who answer women's critical questions in this way, I should like to object: in Church tradition, on the one hand, the masculinity of Jesus is veiled – just think of the furore aroused by uttering or portraying the possibility that Mary Magdalene might have

7. Halkes, *op. cit.*, p.74.

been Jesus's girl friend. The possibility of any form of eroticism triggers off anxiety here. But on the other hand a completely different argument is used: Jesus was a man (here this is suddenly important, and being "human" is inadequate) and the Apostles were men (limiting oneself naturally to the Twelve); therefore only a man can represent Christ in church services, particularly in the celebration of the Eucharist. How is it possible, on the one hand, to emphasize the neutral humanity of Jesus against all those who have problems here, and, on the other, to argue for the malenesss of Jesus when reasons to oppose the ordination of women are required? There are deep-rooted contradictions in this. So many women take exception to the masculine Saviour, and to the elevation of the man Jesus to the role of Pantocrator, as he is depicted over so many church doors. Many have – for other reasons – great difficulties with the ecclesiastical, theological interpretation of his sacrificial death. There is also the problem of the appellation "Lord". Many of us do not use this word in worship any more, and I know ministers, both men and women, who replace the word "Lord" with "God" wherever possible. How do we, as contemporary women and as Christians, handle this question, provided that we are aware of it at all?

There are totally different personal and basic answers to this. The argument that we hear these questions, but that we nevertheless cannot, or will not, free ourselves from the usage with which we have grown up, is part of the personal answer. For example, it is possible to combine a really radical critique of a patriarchal church with a personal faith in Jesus Christ. This does not impinge on the areas that were, and still are, the most significant and sacred in our own history. In my opinion, radical feminists should not be too quick to react with contempt and superciliousness to this attitude, but should rather ask themselves what they themselves exclude from their own thinking. The exreme radical feminist view that such a combination is not possible has been most impressively and significantly expressed by Mary Daly. Those who really wish to get their bearings in this field will have to engage in debate with her, even though this is very challenging. She has reached the conclusion that she should leave the Church. After years of

painful debate, she no longer felt it possible to have faith in
Jesus, or in Christ, or in Jesus Christ. I have already cited the
book in which she basically justifies this attitude, though this
has been superseded by her later ones. Without going into
Mary Daly in more detail here, I must say that I consider her
to be a very significant thinker. She can be accused of
inaccuracies in her bold attempt to combine very disparate
elements in women's history, or criticized for her bold
neologisms, but one cannot simply put her on one side
without learning something from her.

Here I want to restrict myself to two attempts to tackle the
question of Jesus, the Christ. The first is expounded in Hanna
Wolff's, *Jesus der Mann*.[8] Wolff is a theologian and a Jungian
psychologist. She argues that we should not try to skirt round
the humanity of Jesus, but tackle the subject of this man Jesus
in the context of his world, and, of course, using the insights of
modern psychology. Put briefly, Hanna Wolff shows in an
exciting way how the man Jesus stood out against his culture.
This even cost him his life:

> What does this wholly other consist of? How can it be given
> a name? Certainly it has many facets, and we in no way
> maintain . . . that what is named by us is the only aspect, or
> that it includes all the others. We do maintain, however, that
> it is the central aspect for understanding the person of Jesus,
> and it is therefore indispensable: i.e. Jesus is the first man
> who has broken through the androcentricity of the ancient
> world. The despotism of giving value only to what is
> masculine is set aside. Jesus is the first to explode the
> solidarity of men (i.e. of non-integrated men), and their anti-
> feminine or hostile attitude. In Jesus we see the first non-
> hostile man.

By the word "hostile", she understands a person who has not
integrated the side of his or her nature appertaining to the
opposite sex, and who must therefore react with hostility
toward this sex. Thus, in the case of a man, she means the man

---

8. H. Wolff, *Jesus der Mann: der Gestalt Jesu in tiefen-psychologischer Schift*
(Radius Verlag, 1975), pp.80ff.

who has not fully integrated his feminine side, his *anima*, into his life, and so becomes a misogynist. To quote her again: "Hostility, what does this mean? It means everything in the behaviour previously described as belonging to the patriarchal consciousness. The repression of the *anima* corresponds to an outwardly completely anti-feminine approach, the devaluation of what is feminine to 'only feminine', the debasement of feminine values to the level of the demonic, as we have already seen."

Hanna Wolff pursues this line of argument lovingly through the various chapters of her book. She investigates Jesus's encounters with people, especially with women, and demonstrates her awareness of modern New Testament research. So she helps us to build up an image of Jesus through a new approach. She aims further than that, however. She demands of theology that it think through these statements with a new, integrated understanding, as she calls it. Her final argument is: "Theology must resolve to restate the case, to restate it unwaveringly, with an integrated understanding that corresponds to the radical *Novum*, which in fact represents the modern image of human beings developed by depth psychology. That, and that alone, would be a resurrection from theological and ecclesiastical death."

Here, in my opinion, she oversteps the limit she herself previously set; by putting forward a new and absolute demand, which, in my view, does not serve her own argument. As I see it, her interpretation of Jesus the man is a commendable attempt to look at the humanity of Jesus through new eyes. But two things are lacking in this attempt: she ignores what has been made of Jesus in history and theology from the later writings of the New Testament down to the present, which cannot easily be dismissed as a false development. Even after reading this book, I do not know how to approach Jesus the Christ. My second point is connected to the first: her book lacks a feeling for the ultimate mystery of God, a mystery that is hidden somewhere in the form of Christ and also in the Church. I am grateful for what is illuminated by depth psychology, but I must still seek further.

It is difficult to say which direction this search can take. There is a fierce discussion among feminist theologians about the theology of the Cross. Elga Sorge has written very critically on this subject; Elisabeth Moltmann is planning a work on a feminist interpretation of the theology of the Cross. For me personally, the approach taken by Rosemary Radford Ruether and others, namely to attempt to go back to the Jesus of the Synoptic Gospels and his message, is often more helpful. Ruether writes:

> Once the mythology of Jesus the Messiah and divine Logos, with the masculine ideas related to it, is overcome, the Jesus of the Synoptic Gospels is recognizable as a figure remarkably compatible with feminism. This is not to say, unhistorically, that Jesus was a feminist, but rather that the criticism of religious and social hierarchy characteristic of the early portrait of Jesus is remarkably similar to feminist criticism.[9]

Ruether sees in Jesus the fulfilment of the prophetic promise that the humble are raised up, that the existing religious and social hierarchy is not confirmed, but shaken and challenged. If this side of the person, work and message of Jesus is brought out, the way is open for a new understanding of what might be meant by liberation from bondage, oppression and servitude, in both personal and social terms. However, the way will also be open for the word "Christ" to be used again. So it can rightly be said that the human existence of the historical Jesus is ultimately not essential to our faith, but rather that what is meant by the statement "He is the Christ, the Anointed of God" should live on in non-dominating form in the community of those who follow his call in his assembly, his Church, which has continued to pass on his message through the centuries. I should like to quote here again some sentences from Rosemary Radford Ruether, which show me a new way forward.

---

9. Ruether, *Sexism and God-talk*, p.135.

Christ, as the redemptive person and Word of God, is not to be encapsulated "once and for all" in the historical Jesus. The Christian community continues Christ's identity. As vine and branches, Christic personhood continues in our sisters and brothers. In the language of early Christian prophetism, we can encounter Christ in the form of our sisters. Christ, the liberated humanity, is not confined to a static perfection of one person 2000 years ago. Rather, redemptive humanity goes ahead of us, calling us to yet uncompleted dimensions of human liberation.[10]

I am fully aware that these may well be unorthodox ideas. I have tried to be cautious, in the hope of not offending anyone, but of encouraging people to set out together on a path in search of a new language and a new understanding of the central statements of the Christian faith. For me, all this is in a state of flux, and long may it remain so, not only for me, but in the feminist theology movement as a whole.

In conclusion, let me turn briefly to the third Person of he Christian Trinity, the Holy Spirit. He – or she – is possibly the most easily accessible to feminist theology. Many women (and not only women) researchers have drawn attention to the fact that the Hebrew word for spirit, *ruah*, is feminine, that in translation into the Greek *pneuma* it became neuter, and took on a male gender, in grammatical terms, only as the Latin *spiritus*. I can hardly believe that this is merely a word game, once attention is drawn to it. Today attempts are made (with some justification, I think) to devise a feminine form for "spirit". By analogy with other derivations, the word "spiritess" is used. I have resisted using this myself for a long time, and it still irritates me. But if language is a living thing, why shouldn't we create new words? The fact that the three Persons of the Trinity are all male has already disturbed many people. Jung, for example, has suggested that Mary, as a fourth Person, should be incorporated, not into the Trinity, but into a Quaternity. However, let us stay for the moment with the Holy

---

10. *Idem.*, p.148.

Spirit/ess. In the Old Testament, *ruah* is the side of the divine that gives life. At creation, the Spirit (*ruah*) broods over the waters. She is always moving. She is also breath, or the power of life, as in Psalm 104: "When Thou sendest forth Thy Spirit, they are created" (v.30). God then not only creates through his word, but also through the *ruah*. The "wind" spoken of in the vision of Ezekiel (ch. 37) is *ruah*. It is the power that brings the dead, dried-up bones back to life. According to the prophecy of Joel, *ruah*, as the spirit of prophecy, should fall on all people, men and women: "And it will come to pass afterward that I will pour out my spirit, my ruah, on all flesh, and your sons and daughters will prophesy. Your old men will dream dreams, and your young men will see visions. I will even pour out my spirit on the menservants and the maidservants in those days" (Joel 2:28ff.).

In the story of Pentecost, it is said that this prophecy was fulfilled by what happened. This means, then, that the Spirit is closely connected with Jesus as the life-giving power. With the coming of Jesus, the old promise that God's spirit has been poured out on women and men is fulfilled. Here also we can ask once more why this clear statement has had so little effect in the history of the Church.

Reflecting on this life-giving power, women have also discovered a tradition found in the Bible itself, as well as in Gnostic and Apocryphal texts. This is the figure of *sophia*, wisdom, a word I prefer to "spiritess". It is introduced in the Book of Proverbs, where "she" presents herself in the following words:

"The Lord created me at the beginning of his work,
the first of his acts of old.
Ages ago I was set up,
at the first, before the beginning of the earth.
When there were no depths I was brought forth,
when there were no springs abounding with water.
Before the mountains had been shaped,
before the hills, I was brought forth;
before he had made the earth with its fields,
of the first of the dust of the world.

When he established the heavens,
I was there,
when he drew a circle on the face of the deep,
when he made firm the skies above,
when he established the fountains of the deep,
when he assigned to the sea its limit,
so that the waters might not transgress his command,
when he marked out the foundations of the earth,
then I was beside him, like a master workman;
and I was daily his delight,
rejoicing before him always
rejoicing in his inhabited world,
and delighting in the sons of men."

(Proverbs 8:22–31)

The language and style are significantly different from the surrounding text. It is possible, as some feminists have already attempted to discover, that the remains of an old matriarchal culture lie hidden behind the concept of *sophia*. However that may be, to reflect on the Holy Spirit, spirit as power for life and for community (as in the Pentecost story), and to reflect on it in a feminist manner, is also one of the many tasks that lie before us. Interesting examples of this kind of research are to be found in Elaine Pagel's *The Gnostic Gospels*.[11]   Here a woman takes a scholarly look at Gnostic texts, mainly those found in Upper Egypt as late as 1945, and made accessible to the public some years later. This collection reveals a variety of often confusing texts, in which, among other things, wisdom is depicted as the feminine side of God; and the editor examines why these texts were not included in the Canon. Catharina Halkes also says that further theological work lies before us in this area, and in conclusion I should like to quote from her here:

---

11. E. Pagels, *The Gnostic Gospels* (London: Weidenfeld and Nicholson, 1980). [The story of the discovery of these texts and a full account of them is given in Jean Doresse, *The Secret Books of the Egyptian Gnostics* (London: Hollis and Carter, 1960; reprinted Rochester, Vermont: Inner Traditions International, 1986) ED].

Just as I have found little emphasis on pneumatology in pastoral theology, so the Holy Ghost is just as little treated as a subject in the work of feminist theologians. And yet it is my opinion that we must move in this direction. The spirit of Christ, who continues his work among us, appeared when Mary, the Apostles and the women were together, waiting. That was the Ecclesia Church in its authentic form, praying, and receptive to the Spirit who sets them on fire and who is kindled in their lives, as it had previously done in Mary. Then Peter remembers the old prophecy in Joel that all sons and daughters will prophesy. It is amazing how often in ancient religions it is women who were filled by the Spirit and emerged as prophetesses. I regard the feminist movement in its best sense as a challenge to the Church. It is an alien prophecy, which can work as a spiritual movement on the Church, in order to make it a community of men and women in all its forms of expression.[12]

What is being said here is possibly more important than the question of whether *sophia*/wisdom was really the third Person of the Trinity, and has been replaced by the Word and suppressed, yet this question cannot simply be put on one side, since we have to search the Bible for traces of matriarchy as part of our quest, as Christian women, for our own roots.

---

12. C. Halkes, *Gott hat nicht*, p.42.

Chapter 4

Woman – Nature – Spirit

HAVING debated images of God in the last chapter, I should now like to discuss the images that men have made of woman in our church tradition, and how the juxtaposition of men and women, their humanity and their being made in the image of God are interpreted.

I start with a relatively modern declaration, namely the statement made in 1948 in Amsterdam at the formation of the World Council of Churches, that "the Church as the Body of Christ consists of men and women created as responsible persons to glorify God and to do His will", but that "this truth, accepted in theory, is too often ignored in practice." Both parts of this sentence come from the official text of the First World Assembly.[1] It is significant in two respects: the fundamental recognition of an *equality* of men and women (more than equal rights and with a different identity from each other), and the recognition that both were created by God, and both are separately responsible to God. The responsibility of the woman is thus not to be derived from that of the man, nor to be related to it in any way. It is also clear that both are persons. It is thus a far-reaching declaration, but I assume that in no church today would objections be raised to it in this form. We can agree on such a general statement relatively easily. The remarkable thing about it is the second half of the sentence, "that this truth, accepted in theory, is too often ignored in practice". In its original context this statement related to the specific question of the position of women in the service of the Church and in ministry, and led to the first questionnaire to member churches of the WCC. In my opinion, however, the position of women in the service of the Church is only a

---

1. See Kathleen Bliss, *The Service and Status of Women in the Churches*, with a Foreword by W.A. Visser 't Hooft (London: SCM Press, 1952), p.9.

secondary question. The much more fundamental question is
the value placed upon women in the common life of men and
women; this involves the assessment and regulation of the
relations between men and women, and especially the
question of sexuality. We can find ourselves continuing to fight
for centuries for the priesthood of women in all the churches of
the world, if these basic questions of human life together are
not tackled with honesty, or only from a male viewpoint.

I have given a lot of thought to how I should proceed here.
Should I start straightaway with our own times, as Catharina
Halkes does in her remarkable lecture "Women – men –
human beings"?[2] I prefer to follow another route and briefly
examine the teaching and images of some famous theologians
– Augustine, Thomas Aquinas, Martin Luther, Karl Barth – and
put some questions to them. I should like at least to touch on
a part of women's painful history, namely the burning of
witches, and to concern myself with a feminist exegesis of a
biblical text to which these theologians and contemporary
women are always reverting – Genesis 3 – and to draw some
personal conclusions from this. It should be clear that this is
not a random selection, of course, but it is certainly not simply
"objective".

I begin then with Augustine, and inevitably with his
Confessions.[3] This is an exceptionally revealing document for
our subject, because it shows in often startling ways the
struggle of a man for what, in accordance with the assumptions of his time, he understood as chastity. In the Third Book
he writes about the beginning of his student days in
Carthage:

> Although my real need was for you, my God, who are the
> food of the soul, I was not aware of this hunger. I felt no
> need for the food that does not perish, not because I had had
> my fill of it, but because the more I was starved of it, the less
> palatable it seemed. Because of this, my soul fell sick. It
> broke out in ulcers, and looked about desperately for some

2. In C. Halkes, *Suchen was verlorenging* (Siebenstern: GTB, 1977), pp.100ff.
3. St Augustine, *Confessions*, trans. with an Introduction by R.S. Pine-Coffin
(Harmondsworth: Penguin, 1961).

material, worldly means of relieving the itch which they caused. But material things, which have no soul, could not be true objects for my love. To love and to have my love returned was my heart's desire, and it would be all the sweeter if I could also enjoy the body of the one who loved me. So I muddied the stream of friendship with the filth of lewdness and clouded its clear waters with Hell's black river of lust. And yet, in spite of this rank depravity, I was vain enough to have ambitions of cutting a fine figure in the world. I also fell in love, which was a snare of my own choosing. . . .[4]

And in the Eighth Book: "As a youth, I had been woefully at fault, particularly in early adolescence. I had prayed to You for chastity, and said, 'Give me chastity and continence, but not yet.' For I was afraid that You would answer my prayer at once and cure me too soon of the disease of lust, which I wanted satisfied, not quelled."[5]

The subject is obvious: sexual desire, which he cannot master, stands for him in opposition to knowledge of God, which he seeks so ardently. Even though Augustine grappled critically with the dualistic teaching of the Manichees, rejecting their doctrine that sexuality is sinful in itself, one still finds in his *Confessions* the separation of spirit from nature that has had such a disastrous effect throughout the whole history of the Church, right up to the present day. Not that I want to make Augustine responsible for this; here too the connotations are much more complicated and diverse. I quote him only as an influential witness, and even when he says in the first passage quoted that he could not love something that had no soul, and we can discern behind this the desire for total experience, this illusion is immediately destroyed, when he describes his desire to possess the body of the beloved as darkness and Hell's depravity.

Let us now take a look at how, with this background, Augustine treated the woman whom he actually wanted to

---

4. *Ibid.*, III/1, p.55.
5. *Ibid.*, VIII/7, p. 169.

marry – marriage in his time representing the only possibility
of consecrating and taming the otherwise abominable sexual
ardour. He writes in the Sixth Book of the *Confessions*:

> Meanwhile I was sinning more and more. The woman with
> whom I had been living was torn from my side as an
> obstacle to my marriage, and this was a blow which crushed
> my heart to bleeding, because I loved her dearly. She went
> back to Africa (i.e. from Rome), vowing never to give herself
> to any other man, and left with me the son whom she had
> borne me. But I was too unhappy and too weak to imitate
> this example set to me by a woman. I was impatient at the
> delay of two years which had to pass before the girl whom
> I had asked to marry became my wife, and because I was
> more a slave of lust than a true lover of marriage, I took
> another mistress, without the sanction of wedlock . . ."[6]

The exact circumstances of the separation are not known, but
I think the story speaks for itself, particularly the fact that the
name of this woman is not given one single time in the
Confessions. He "took" the one and then the other. What
became of this woman apparently bothered him as little as the
fate of the next mistress he took. The son was called
Adeodatus. A remarkable mixture of respect and contempt
speaks in these sentences, in that he himself admits he could
not follow the example of this woman who vowed never to
give herself to another man.

As Augustine presents his life as being well-pleasing to God,
he describes his eventual conversion as follows:

> I could see the chaste beauty of Continence in all her serene
> unsullied joy, as she modestly beckoned me to cross over
> and to hesitate no more. She stretched out loving hands to
> welcome and embrace me, holding up a host of good
> examples to my sight. With her were countless boys and
> girls, great numbers of the young and people of all ages,
> staid widows and women still virgins in old age. And in
> their midst was Continence herself, not barren, but a fruitful

---

6. *Ibid.*, VI/15, p.131.

mother of children of joys borne of you, O Lord, her spouse.[7]

The images are revealing, and so is the language: virgins, widows, and Continence as the spiritual mother of many children. Joy, desire and unsullied happiness are despised, there is nothing beyond earnest serenity and propriety. Another quotation – the last – from another work of Augustine's fits this picture: "We ought not to condemn wedlock because of the evil of lust, nor must we praise lust because of the good of wedlock."[8]

I must, as a woman, see behind such statements the countless women who were never asked about their feelings, who because of male desire often had to bear far too many children (and still have to), who were "taken", and then discarded, sent or thrown away. I should like to say once more: I do not blame Augustine alone for this; his struggle for a living faith and his struggle with God impress me. But it disturbs me that, because of him, sin was so strongly linked to sexuality, which according to my deepest convictions is un-biblical, and it also disturbs me that when men couple sin with sexuality, woman is debased – explicity or implicitly – whether she is now the temptress or simply the means to an end, whether of slaking men's desire or of producing the next generation.

Now we make a great leap from the fourth and fifth centuries to the thirteenth. This was the age of the trouba-dours, who, in wonderful ballads, sang of the noble lady, usually unattainable. It was also the age of scholasticism. Thomas Aquinas paid close attention to the nature of man and woman. A committed Roman Catholic, Gertrud Heinzelmann,

---

7. *Ibid.*, VIII/11, p.176.
8. From "De nupt. et concup." I/8, in D.S. Bailey, *The Man-woman Relation in Christian Thought* (Harlow: Longman, 1959), p.56. Bailey summarizes Augustine's thought: "As concupiscence cannot take away the good of marriage, neither can marriage mitigate the evil of concupiscence, but it can serve to moderate venial desire, and to divert it harmlessly and usefully to the task of procreation. Wedded chastity in fact consists in transforming coitus from a satisfaction of lust to a necessary duty, and when the act is employed for generation it is excused of its inherent sinfulness."

has, in her contribution to the Second Vatican Council, concerned herself with the discourses of the great Church Father on this subject. They are frankly contradictory, as well as exceptionally recondite and abstruse for people today.[9] The important aspect of them here is that he debased women in contrast to men. His most quoted statement is that the procreation of a woman is a mistake, that she is an incomplete man, and her only vocation is to serve the ends of reproduction. In this, she is the material. Man, as the active part, gives it form. "In procreation, the mother provides the formless matter; this takes on its form, by which it becomes a being, from the formative power in the father's semen. And although this power cannot create the rational soul, yet it prepares the material to take on this kind of nature."

Even for Aquinas himself it is clear that woman cannot be denied a rational soul, created by God, which is why women are always baptised. Obviously, the lack of biological knowledge of the role of the woman's ovum at this time determined many of the judgments of this Church Father. But when one reads through his statements, the impression grows still stronger: an anxious, intelligent, unmarried man collects together all the natural and biblical reasons to justify the existing subordination of woman in the Church, and to make it appear reasonable. Presumably his thoughts, difficult of access to us, hardly reached the laity even then, but the debasement of woman and sexuality to which they led, the interpretation of marriage as a means of salvation, in which every aspect of a relationship between the marriage partners is omitted, the praise of virginity as the highest state, the clear condemnation of all sexual sins have without doubt affected the position of both men and women over the centuries.

A significant fact which also says something about the attitude of men to women is the half-hearted approval of prostitution in Augustine as well as in Aquinas. The argument is interesting: prostitution is something like pollution in the

---

9. G. Heinzelmann, *Wir schweigen nicht länger* (Zurich: Feminas Verlag, 1962).

sea or a sewage system in a palace. If this is removed, the palace overflows with sewage. Aquinas argues as follows:

> Human dominion is derived from divine dominion and should emulate it. Now God, although He is almighty and the highest good, allows certain evils which he could prevent to exist in the universe, so that without them no greater good is realized or greater evil arises. Correspondingly, in human dominion those who govern are right to tolerate certain evils, in order that certain good things are not lost or certain greater evils appear. . . . Banish prostitutes from the world and you will fill it with sodomy. For this reason, Augustine says in Book XIII of *De Civitate Dei* that the secular state has made recourse to prostitutes a justifiable immorality (*licitam turpitudinem*).[10]

The higher good that needs to be preserved is marriage and also the virtue and purity of "respectable" women. What happened to prostitutes apparently did not disturb these theologians in the slightest. Man's untameable instinct, despised of course, but regarded as being given by nature, justified their existence. It should not be too difficult to trace these lines of thought down to our own time, when the focus of attention is directed at the fate of women, particularly those in South-East Asia, who are either misused in sex tourism in their own country, or are imported into the industrial countries. At least hardly any theologian would now justify this openly.

Now one might think that during the Reformation period the debasement of women was overcome by the abolition of celibacy in the churches that adopted the new teaching. But this was not so, even if much was undoubtedly changed by the actual fact of clerical matrimony and the participation of wives in the debates over the new teaching. The extent to which the subordination of woman to man and her concentration on motherhood survived, can be shown by some passages from a sermon by Martin Luther and his commentary on Genesis. He took it for granted that a woman should have as many

---

10. *Summa Theologiae*, II-II, 10, 11.

children as possible. These children were valued as a blessing from God, just as the woman's suffering in pregnancy and childbirth was considered just punishment for Eve's fall. If the woman accepted this suffering in faith, then she fulfilled the work God had assigned to her. As an illustration, here are a few sentences from a sermon of Luther's in 1525:

> For this reason one should warn women travailing in childbirth to show all possible diligence, that is, devote all their power and might so that the child is delivered, even if they die in the effort. . . . So one should also comfort and strengthen a woman in childbirth . . .; my dear woman, consider that you are a woman, and that this work in you is pleasing to God; take comfort joyfully in His will, and let Him have His right over you; pray for the child, and do that with all your might; if you should die, then you will go in the name of God; it is well with you, for you truly die in a noble work and in obedience to God. Yes, my dear woman, if you were not a woman, for the sake of this work alone, you should desire that you were a woman, and so endure these precious sufferings and even die in God's work and purpose; for here is God's Word that has created you, and has sown such travail within you. . . .

The actual bible text referred to here (and elsewhere) is 1 Timothy 2:11–15: "Let a woman learn in silence with all submissiveness, for I do not allow a woman to teach, also not to raise herself above the man, but (I pray her) to keep silent. For Adam was created first, afterwards Eve. And Adam was not tempted, the woman was tempted and became a trans-gressor. But she shall be saved by childbearing, if she remains in faith and love and holiness with modesty." Luther ex-pounded this deutero-Pauline text with a truly masculine exhortation to women.

It was just as obvious to him that the woman must submit herself to the man, and this submission is justified either by the curse on woman (Gen. 3:16) or follows from the way she was created. On this point, here are a few more sentences in the same vein from Luther's commentary on this text from 1 Timothy 3:

Paul thus has proved that by divine and human right Adam is the master of the woman. That is, it was not Adam who went astray. Therefore there was greater wisdom in Adam than in the woman.... Adam sinned knowingly, but he wanted to agree with his wife and please her.... He presses the idea that Satan did not attack Adam.... The serpent did not deceive Adam because it did not tempt him by speaking with him, therefore Paul is correct in saying Adam was deceived not by the serpent but by the woman.... She became the cause of transgression. Paul uses the argument that we have in Genesis 3, v.16: "Because you have done this, you will be under the man. In punishment for your sin and transgression, you must be subject to the man and suffer the pains of childbirth." Thus that ordinance of God continues to stand as a memorial of that transgression by which her fault entered into the world.[11]

The fact that the woman looked after the household was held to derive from this. In Luther's exegesis of Genesis, written between 1536 and 1545, he writes:

The rule remains with the husband, and the wife is compelled to obey him by God's command. He rules the home and the state, wages wars, defends his possessions, tills the soil, builds, plants, etc. The woman, on the other hand, is like a nail driven into the wall. She sits at home, and for this reason Paul, in Titus 2 v. 5 calls her a "keeper in the house". The pagans have depicted her as Venus, standing on a seashell, for just as a snail carries its house with it, so the wife should stay at home and look after the affairs of the household, as one who has been deprived of the ability of administering those affairs that are outside and that concern the state. She does not go beyond her most personal duties.[12]

11. Jaroslav Pelikan, ed., *Luther's Works*, vol. 28. Sermons on 1 Corinthians 7, 1 Corinthians 15; lectures on 1 Timothy (St Louis: Concordia, 1973), pp. 278–9.
12. *Ibid.*, vol. 1. Lectures on Genesis 1–5, p.203.

Women apparently rebelled against this already in Luther's own time. He notes with disapproval in the same Commentary that the wives "enjoy evil and are impatient" and "by nature strive for what they have lost through sin". Thus there was already a women's movement even in those days.

If one compares these texts with those of Augustine and Thomas Aquinas, one has to say that they are at least closer to reality. The wrestling with desire, experienced with good conscience in marriage, has actually disappeared here. But for the woman little has changed. It is obvious that she has to bear the consequences, and she gets her just deserts when she has to suffer the pain of many births. In this way, she fulfils God's will. In a later age, Count Zinzendorf, the founder of the Moravian Church, comforted his wife with the information that she should not be sad over the deaths of the children she had borne, since they were with the Lord.

What is still there in Luther is the clear subordination of woman and the division of work between man and woman, according to God's will, all to be decided by men – just as even today men still want to decide, and do decide, whether a woman wants to bear and can bear a child.

The last man in this series to whom I should like to give a voice is Karl Barth, who in his *Church Dogmatics*, in his anthropology as much as in his ethics, comments on the distinction between man and woman in a very interesting and surprising way. He derives this from Genesis 1 and 2 and the Song of Songs, with references to God's Covenant with Israel and the passages in the Pauline Epistles that speak of man being the head and of the reciprocal mutuality of man and woman, as well as to Ephesians 5:21ff, where similarly the man-woman relationship is seen in the light of the relationship of Christ to his community. I can refer to only a few basic principles here, and I am aware that I am not doing justice to Barth's work. (I am indebted for these important references to an unpublished study of this aspect of Barth's anthropology by a young woman. The unfortunate fact of this work remaining unpublished is part of the theme of this book – "women remain invisible".)

Barth proceeds without any consideration of textual criticism of the two creation narratives. He sees the culmination of these narratives in the creation of mankind in the image of God (Gen. 1:27). It is introduced with the striking sentence: "And God said: Let us create man in our own image." None of the earlier creation events is introduced so emphatically and in such a solemn way. Clearly this refers to something special, different from the creation of the universe and of the plant and animal kingdoms previously narrated. Yet Barth sees much more in this. According to him, the plural "let us" is not simply a solemn introduction, nor the "royal 'we' ", which in his opinion does not exist in the Old Testament (something that I cannot check), but instead is to be interpreted as intra-divine self-communication. "In God's own being and sphere there is a counterpart: a genuine but harmonious self-encounter and self-discovery: a free co-existence and co-operation, and open confrontation and reciprocity."[13]

For Barth it is an important and fundamental concept that God is not solitary in himself, and by creating mankind as his image ("our" image) he creates a counterpart to himself, but he also creates this mankind as a counterpart to "I and Thou": "Thus the *tertium comparationis*, the analogy between God and man, is simply the existence of the I and Thou in confrontation. This is the first constitutive for God, and then for man created by God."[14]

I cannot and do not want to enter here into discussion of the justification and theological basis for this argument; I only want to describe the train of thought that has undoubtedly strongly influenced a whole generation of theologians.

The next step proceeds from the Creation narrative that says: "God created them male and female". If we follow Barth, this is then the human confrontation underlying everything. Races, peoples, etc., are not mentioned in Genesis 1, but only this distinction between man and woman: "Man is no more solitary than God. But as God is One, and as He alone is God, so man as man is One and alone, and two only in the duality

---

13. K. Barth, *Church Dogmatics*, III, 1., *Doctrine of Creation* (Edinburgh: T. & T. Clark, 1958), p.185.
14. *Ibid.*

of his own kind, in the duality of man and woman. In this way he is a copy and imitation of God. In this way he repeats in his confrontation of God and himself the confrontation in God."[15]

These human beings are placed together under God's blessing, and destined for dominion over the rest of Creation and for the propagation of the human race. This divine command should be fulfilled in the life of human beings and in accordance with God's order. So it would appear that this human being is not only created in God's image, but also that he must always view things from this perspective. It will also be shown that even the "incident" of the Fall cannot nullify God's blessing. "It will be shown that man has reason to look for the man who will be different from him, but who for this reason will be real man for him, in the image and likeness of God, male and female, in his place and on his behalf, namely Jesus Christ and his community. The history of the Covenant, whose beginning, centre and goal will be this man – this man and this woman – will confirm the history of Creation, and thus confirm the blessing given to man."[16]

Barth does not stop, however, with the first Creation narrative, as many of us women would gladly do, but he turns equally lovingly to Genesis 2, where, as is well known, the creation of woman is represented as being from the rib of Adam, a prior creation. Barth's train of thought is very interesting here, too. For him the climax of the passage is the man's exclamation, when the woman stands before him: "This at last". This is preceded by the parade of all the animals in front of the still solitary man. He has to name them, but in none of them can he recognize an "opposite number", who corresponds to him. Therefore God causes him to fall into a deep sleep, takes a rib from him, closes up the wound, and makes a woman out of the rib. The deep sleep shows that Adam is not involved in the creation of the woman. Barth also says that God inflicted a wound on him, so that henceforward he lacks something (so he is after all involved with a part of

15. *Ibid.*, p.186.
16. *Ibid.*, p.190.

himself, but not actively), and when the woman stands before him, he exclaims in recognition: "Here she is" – "This at last", "flesh of my flesh and bone of my bone". He gives her the name Ischa, "female man". What is meant by this is a profound relationship of belonging together. The word "help" (or "helpmeet", as it is often incorrectly translated) is paraphrased by Barth as "help, who is a counterpart to him". In this formulation it is easy to see the train of thought going back to Genesis 1. Moreover, it is said that God provided her for the man. He accepts his counterpart from God's hand. By assenting to this, he assents to the fulfilment of his own creation; previously it had been: "It is not good that man should be alone."

In the following remarks on the community of man and woman, Barth takes a good look at what this belonging together means now for man and woman:

> The point of the name given by the saga is that woman is of man. This does not mean that she is really mannish. Nor does it mean that she is man's property. Nor does it mean that unlike him she is not a human being in the full sense. What it does mean is that in her being and existence she belongs to him; that she is ordained to be his helpmeet; that without detriment to her independence, she is the part of him which was lost and is found again – "taken out of him". It is proper to her to be beside him.[17]

Barth maintains that this relation is not reciprocal, and not reversible. He also maintains the supremacy of the man, but this is

> ... not a question of value, dignity or honour, but of order. It does not denote a higher humanity of man. Its acknowledgement is no shame to woman. On the contrary, it is an acknowledgement of her glory, which in a particular and decisive respect is greater even than that of man. Again from the standpoint of this passage, we can only say that those who do not know woman in this relationship to man do not

---

17. *Ibid.*, p.301.

know her at all. A whole host of masculine and feminine
reflections concerning woman completely miss her reality,
because this element is either not taken into consideration at
all, or is not taken into consideration properly.[18]

Here, if not earlier, I begin to find the argument problematic,
and it becomes even more so when the woman is described as
the "chosen" of the man. The language is deceptively
comparable with the customary expression, that the man
chooses and the woman is "the chosen one". It becomes even
more problematic when in the next volume of his *Church
Dogmatics* Barth adopts the concept of the stronger being of the
man and the weaker being of the woman, and yet somehow
relates it to what he has said above, and also when he says:

> There can be no question that man is to woman and woman
> is to man supremely the other, the fellow-man, to see and to
> be seen by whom, to speak with and to listen to whom, to
> receive from and to render assistance to whom is necessarily
> a supreme human need and problem and fulfilment, so that
> whatever may take place between man and man and
> woman and woman is only as it were a preliminary and
> accompaniment for this true encounter between man and
> fellow-man, for this true being in fellow-humanity.[19]

Elsewhere he says that this is fulfilled in the love and marriage
of man and woman in the way that best corresponds to God's
intention.

Here I should like to insert a personal comment. I have never
been a Barthian, but I worked on this part of Barth's *Dogmatics*
intensively when I was a student, and later on. I still vividly
remember the great relief I felt when I read Barth's formulation, "This at last", for the first time, and also his indissoluble
counterpart-relationship of man and woman, and for years I
adopted the phrase, "help who is a counterpart to him", even
as a single woman. In another place Barth reduces the
emphasis he placed solely on marriage. For many women of

18. *Ibid.*, pp.301–2.
19. *Ibid.*, II, 2, p.288.

my generation these expressions, together with those of
leading Old Testament scholars such as Gerhard von Rad and
Walter Zimmerli were the first approaches to an alternative –
as we experienced it – consideration of man and woman,
taking partnership seriously, something for which we worked
and hoped, not only with regard to marriage, but also to
relationships in the workplace. I should not like to have
missed these experiences. They became alive for me as I went
back again to these passages. Yet I have other questions today:
Are we actually seen here as real women? Are not these
expressions, which speak of partnership, wishful thinking by a
man who constructed a wonderful, self-contained system, in
which "the woman" was one small ingredient? Of course, we
know that Karl Barth had worked out these ideas not in the
first place with his wife, but with his colleague, Charlotte von
Kirschbaum. Was she perhaps a "help in counterpart", a
helpmeet who, in spite of all their openness, always remained
in the shadows? In the end, one more invisible woman . . .

I have provided sketches of the images of women in the work
of significant theologians. They vary considerably, but they
have one thing in common. It is men, men living in patriarchy,
who create these images. They all see themselves in a superior
position, they are all convinced that this position is God's will,
they all fall back on the Creation narratives or sagas for
justification, and they all show, at least in their speech, that
their actual position in the church and society of their time,
that is, their experience as men in patriarchy, has moulded
these images. If we women realize this, must we always
accept it as God's way of ordering things?
    We have already come to the conclusion that all these
models of the counterpart, of the mutual relationship, of the
assignment of woman to man, represent a form of subordination or secondary status for woman, or at best an extension of
man through woman, (which is indeed a form of secondary
status – he is there, she is "assigned" to him). They were all
dual models; the duality of man and woman was understood
as the basic model of human intercourse, of human relationships. As Catharina Halkes says in the article "Women – Men

– Human beings" already quoted: "Dual models" belong "to a hierarchical society, in which an upper stratum of powerful men has the say." She is of the opinion – and I agree with her – that these dual models do not basically contain what Jesus himself willed and lived. He, the true image of God, called men and women to his service, not in pairs, but as persons, and his community was not based on marriage and family, but was a completely different kind of community, with a unique character. I should like to return later to this idea.

First, let us look deeper into the question of dual models. The dualism of man and woman, given as part of creation, and corrupted by the Fall but in no way abandoned, has, in the history of the Church, led to man being equated with spirit, and woman with nature and the flesh. A further perversion followed closely on this: that woman was evil incarnate for man. Think of Augustine's struggle with evil desire and his dealings with women resulting from this. This identification of woman with evil is supported by interpretations of Genesis 3, the story of the so-called "Fall". We have already had a foretaste of this in the passages from Martin Luther. Rosemary Radford Ruether rightly states that Genesis 3 by no means plays such an important role in the context of the Old Testament or in Jewish tradition, as it does in our Christian tradition. Certainly, in our Christian tradition this story or saga has always been interpreted in such a way that the woman was seen as the temptress. This temptation was then "naturally" interpreted sexually, and blame for the Fall was laid on her. This in its turn had the disastrous consequence that the Fall as such came under the spell of sexuality. This is deduced from the approach to the Tree of Knowledge in the narrative. Total knowledge and sexuality definitely have something to do with each other – feminist theology maintains this very point – but this was not understood in this way in the framework of the "dual model" in our tradition. Rather, with the confirmation of the role of woman as temptress, a dangerous division of spirit from body came to be generally accepted. The first signs of this dogma are to be found already in the New Testament, most clearly in the deutero-Pauline Epistle 1 Timothy, where the prohibition on women teaching is justified as follows: "Because Adam was created first, then Eve. And Adam was not deceived, the woman was rather deceived and became a transgressor" (1 Tim. 2:13ff). This passage definitely does not come from Paul himself, since where he concerns himself with the Fall in Romans 5, he speaks of Adam as the prototype of human beings, and he clearly does not see the Fall as to do with sex or sexuality. It is not Adam the man, but Adam the human being. Unfortunately, as so often in the history of the Church, the passage that discriminates against women has carried far greater weight. The most severe and best-known statement of this kind comes from a Church Father, Tertullian: *"You* are the Devil's gateway. *You* are the unsealer of that forbidden tree. *You* are the first deserter of the divine law. *You* are she who persuaded him whom the Devil was not valiant enough to attack. *You* destroyed so easily God's image, man. On account of *your* desert, that is death, even the Son of Man had to die" (*de Cult. Fem.* 1.1.). [Italics by R.R. Ruether][20]

It is easy to say that no one today seriously considers this to be true; this may well be the case, but there is a reality behind such expressions, namely the contempt men have for women, which continues even today, contempt to the point of violence, of rape of body, soul and mind. Ultimately this derives from failure to integrate sexuality in all its facets, and the Church shares this guilt to the highest degree. If I deal here more with men than with women, the reason is that I really believe that they have greater problems in this respect, but above all, because they still always have "the say", and their attitude, especially in the Church, has had particularly fatal consequences, for themselves and for us women. The projection of masculine fears and masculine wishes on to women has had a disastrous effect, because of the different positions they occupy within a hierarchical society. Yet precisely because of this, it is a call to women and men to devote themselves to the reappraisal of long-neglected and taboo topics, particularly in the Church.

---

20. Tertullian quoted in Ruether, *Sexism and God-talk*, p.167.

In connection with this subject, I recently re-discoverd the autobiography of Hannah Tillich, *From Time to Time*. She was the wife of the great theologian Paul Tillich. She describes her life with him, as well as with other men, and his life with her, as well as with other women. What particularly shocked me about this was that the great theologian occupied himself in his spare time with pornography, not for the purpose of study, but for its own sake, and indeed in the way that adolescents do: covering the pornographic pictures with a "respectable" book, which hid them from the eyes of others. What chasms there yawn between the offical theology, set down in books, and daily and nightly existence! I am not saying this in a moralistic way; I am not full of moral indignation; I am just speechless at the non-integration of the dark side of the life of such an important theologian. His wife calls him "King Midas of the Spirit", who turned everything he had not been able to cope with into the "gold of abstraction". Herein lies the tragedy of a man who wanted to develop (or, perhaps had to develop) only one side of himself – the intellectual side – to the neglect of everything else. Who knows which it was? But the tension between spirit and nature described above, and the division of roles between men and women, and the "pure", exclusively masculine theology promoted, protected and stylized by the Church, all must have had something to do with it.

The projection of what was repressed became historical reality in a truly catastrophic way in the persecution of witches. These occupy a very marginal position in the official historiography of the Church as well as of secular history. Obviously they are meant to be described as a marginal phenomenon of very limited significance, or even not described at all, an aberration of superstition in the dark past. Incidentally, this "dark past" belongs especially to the fifteenth, sixteenth and seventeenth centuries, i.e. the time of the Renaissance, of Humanism, of the Reformation. . . . Nobody knows exactly how many witches were condemned, tortured and burned. The overwhelming majority of them were women. Estimates vary between several hundred thousand and nine million. So we are dealing with a veritable holocaust.

Women who are looking into their own history today have researched this question; this is possible, because precise reports exist of the trials that took place in accordance with the procedures laid down. They were carried out with the same precision as the so-called "final solution" to the Jewish question in our century.

In this connection, both the attitude of the Church and the identity of the victims are of interest. Typically, the witches were accused of sexual impurity: "All witchcraft comes from carnal lust which in women is insatiable",[21] according to the Dominican priests Kramer and Sprenger, the authors of the *Malleus Maleficarum*, which appeared in 1486 and contained a catalogue of possible offences. It was thus Christian men, priests and theologians, who compiled the arguments as to why witches, primarily women, should be condemned and executed. In their arguments they drew particularly on the theologians we have previously discussed. Thomas Aquinas and Augustine were, according to Mary Daly, most frequently quoted, and the trials conducted by both the inquisitors, Kramer and Sprenger, were expressly sanctioned by the then Pope, Innocent VIII. The women were accused of copulation with the Devil, of castrating men by magical arts, of murdering children and so on: male projections, reflecting male anxieties and sexual fantasies. These fantasies could be lived out in the torture of women.

Witches were accused of transgressing directly against God's majesty. Stamping them out was supposed to cleanse the Body of Christ. Heretics had to be cut off from this Body like diseased members. This was carried out, not only by the Church acting alone, but with the powerful support of the state, and it did not take place only in the Catholic Church. I will briefly quote what Jean Bodin, a learned French jurist and political theorist, said on this subject in the sixteenth century: "But those greatly err who think that penalties are established only to punish crime. I hold that this is the least of the fruits which accrue to the state. For the greatest and the chief is the

---

21. See Mary Daly, *Gyn/Ecology: the Meta-ethics of Radical Feminism* (Boston: Beacon Press, 1978; London: The Women's Press, 1979), p.180.

appeasing of the wrath of God, especially if the crime is directly against the majesty of God, as is this one. . . ."[22]

Who were these women then? Frequently, they were those who did not fit into the system of the patriarchal family, i.e. single women or widows, but there were also women who displayed supernatural powers as healers or midwives. In every case they were independent women, who, on the one hand, inspired trust (among women whom they could support and heal), and, on the other hand, anxiety, especially among men in the Church, who suspected demonic powers. It could well be possible that remnants of a matriarchal religion were handed on from woman to woman. The persecutors were educated men, but naturally not the torturers themselves. It is still often the case today that those who advance an argument are not the same people as those who carry out the action advocated. On this point, another quotation from Mary Daly:

> In studying the witchcraze, then, we see that the victimizers belonged to a "higher" class of men, in the sense that they had professional legitimation and officially recognized knowledge. If we examine the status of the victims, it is clear that these women were not necessarily from the higher social and economic classes, but that they constituted a threat to the rising professional hierarchy precisely as possessors of (unlegitimated) higher learning, that is, of spiritual wisdom and healing – and of the highly independent character that accompanies such wisdom.[23]

I must break off this line of argument here, and one may ask why I made this excursus at all. I did so for two reasons. First, I wanted to show how lines of thought can be derived from a dual model, so outwardly harmless, which implies ideas ranging from subordination to discrimination against women. Of course this does not mean that this is inevitable, but it does show what can happen, what has happened, and what is also happening today, when one includes the many varied forms of

---

22. *Ibid.*, p.182.
23. *Ibid.*, p.195.

violence against women. Of course, I also know that violence by men against men exists, and that women can use or take part in violence against other women. Reality cannot be explained by referring to only one cause, but here I am concerned with what I regard as *one* very important line. Secondly, I made this excursus out of solidarity with our sisters in earlier ages, because I wanted to make at least a small contribution toward exposing a falsification of history, and to bring into the light a phenomenon that has been suppressed.[24]

I now want to return to my original starting point. While in the whole area of the connection between man, woman and nature I have referred continually to the original biblical narrative, I should now like, in contrast to the interpretations and systems worked out by men, to review a feminine interpretation, not of the Creation narrative, but of Genesis 3, the story of the Fall, and, on this basis, to reach a personal conclusion. In her book *Religion und Frau*,[25] Elga Sorge has produced a very interesting and consistently feminine interpretation of Genesis 3: "The drama of the Fall as the downfall of the Goddess and her Hero". She starts from the premise that one is dealing with a myth here, and that this story can be adequately understood only when the mythic symbols, the ancient symbols under the patriarchal layer, are revealed, un-covered. In her view, this myth has been historicized in the interests of a change that took place at the time the Book of Genesis was written. This was during the reign of King Solomon, when the monarchy was still recent and not yet firmly established. Israel was changing from a nomadic people into a well-structured state. According to Sorge, part of this process was the "bureaucratization and hierarchization of all spheres of life, as well as the reinforcing or developing of hierarchical relations between

---

24. Readers interested in exploring this subject more deeply are recommended to read at least the relevant chapter from Mary Daly's book cited above. She also provides references to the primary sources she has used.
25. E. Sorge, *Religion und Frau; weibliche Spiritualität im Christentum* (Stuttgart: Kolhammer, 1985).

men and women." (Incidentally, it is said of Solomon in the
Old Testament that he had seven hundred wives and three
hundred concubines [I Kgs 11:3] – told not critically but with
admiration.) In this time of change, the patriarchal re-
interpretation of elements stemming from a matriarchal
culture took place, and was handed down to us. So, according
to Sorge, the figure of Eve, who is treated much more as an
independent person than Adam in the Jahwist narrative, is a
survival of the primeval mother or the great goddess. When,
after the Fall, Adam gives her the name "the mother of all
living things" (Genesis 3:20), this is her rightful name. This is
what she really is. But by bestowing this name on her, he
assumed lordship over her. The dethroning of the Great
Mother, the Mother of all living things, goes hand in hand with
robbing woman of her rights. It is quite clear that at this time,
as is well documented by the Old Testament, Israel was
waging a bitter struggle against the cult of the goddess, the
goddesses of fertility, as they were generally called. Basically,
in Sorge's interpretation, the original myth sought to say that,
in giving Adam the apple, Eve wanted to give him a share in
her power of love, and in her deep knowledge of life and love.
Love and knowledge belong together, which the woman
knows better, and the apple was a love apple from the
Paradise of the Goddess. Incidentally, as Sorge points out,
there are pictures in existence of the Madonna giving the child
Jesus an apple – for example, the well-known Madonna by
Matthias Grünewald in Stuppach.

Unprejudiced contemporary women readers of the Bible,
free of tradition, have discovered for themselves, as I did, that
in this account Eve is more active, more independent and
bolder, and they accordingly value Adam the less. Sorge rejects
this last idea, firstly because she does not want to replace the
devaluation of woman in patriarchy by a devaluation of man.
But secondly, because it does not accord with the myth of the
goddess and her hero. The original Adam was the man who
let himself be initiated by the woman into her wisdom of love
and life. Naturally under the historical conditions already
described, this could not survive. King Solomon was regarded
as the absolutely ideal image of the male king, with whom all

his successors strove to identify themselves. Why then is Adam presented in the story of the Fall as somewhat inferior? He is not made to carry the chief burden of guilt; in this way he becomes the pitiful victim of the temptress Eve, and his conduct is even praised, when it is said to the woman: "Thy desire shall be to thy husband, and he shall rule over thee." A remarkable mixture, which Elga Sorge opposes (in my opinion, correctly), but which, as she says, very many women have adopted as an interpretation of their own dependency, have adopted as God given, and so as a real punishment. This distorts the original meaning of the myth. The man does not let himself be led by the woman into a life of love, which can be lived without violence and the need for repression, and the original goddess is not only subordinated to her lord, but also "from now on she is to interpret her creative joy in child-bearing as a punishment from this God. Her ability to bear children, which hitherto gave her worth and power, becomes a snare, which delivers her up to the man; because from now on he reproduces himself through her, and degrades the woman to an instrument of his fertility."[26]

Conventional masculine theology does not share this view of the Fall. As we have already seen, in the masculine system presented above, the independent role of Eve is merely used for attributing to her full responsibility for the act of sinning.

There still remains the role of the serpent. Most commentators hardly refer to it any more, or attach little importance to it. It is simply there, and personifies evil in some way. Sorge also sees in the serpent an ancient symbol of female fertility and cleverness. The serpent, which sheds its skin yearly, is, like the moon, a symbol of the eternal return of life and the cyclic life of women. Basically the story of the Fall could be called the story of the Serpent's Fall. She speaks of: " . . . the downfall of a nature-loving religion, which implies the loss of rights and power for women, and the setting up of a male-dominated religion, which assimilates feminine elements and subordinates them. . . . Feminine wisdom, which the serpent symbol-

---

26. *Ibid.*, p.103.

izes, is cursed by Jahweh. This symbolic act leaves nothing to be desired in interpretation."[27]

God figures in this story as the one who erects prohibitions and imposes punishments, and before whom one must justify oneself, which leads Adam into seeking to attribute Eve's guilt to the serpent. The punishment is banishment from Paradise. Sorge thinks that patriarchy has no clear visions of life in Paradise, whereas the matriarchal Paradise once really existed, and exists in certain forms right up to the present. She draws certain conclusions about the subject of myth from her ideas, here presented in very abbreviated form: "So there are nowadays two issues: to present the goddess to advantage, and at the same time a women-loving, life-loving and Eros-loving spirituality, which recognizes the holiness of life; and to humanize the God of law, to enliven him and to set him in an appropriate relation to the overarching divine wisdom, which created this God."[28]

One could take the easy way out and say that Elga Sorge goes too far, or that at best she borrows various lines of argument only hinted at in this passage; that her interpretations are not credible, are based upon untenable premises. But could that not be said with equal justification about male interpretations of these texts? These, though, are determined by premises we perhaps trust more because we are used to them and have grown up with them, but which nonetheless fail to stand up to a non-patriarchal critique. Elga Sorge at least declares her own viewpoint, her own interests and presuppositions, in unequivocal terms. However, the question remains: What do we make of her, what do I make of her?

I can give only a very provisional answer. On the one hand, I welcome her attempt to expose a layer that has, without question, been suppressed in Christian tradition, in the systems built up by men. On the other hand, I wonder whether a new system is not being erected with this myth of the goddess and her hero, one that we must now look for and

---

27. *Ibid.*, pp.107ff.
28. *Ibid.*, p.111.

find traces of everywhere. The least provisional issue for me is that the rape of nature, of women, and therefore of a side of people, even of men, by patriarchy, is clearly brought out and proved. The existence of a matriarchy before patriarchal culture is also something that cannot be denied, and I should like to know more about it. I do not doubt the seriousness of research in this area. Whether and how this is to be further stimulated, I do not know. I also wonder whether a new dual model is being constructed here – the Goddess and her Hero. Certainly, it is not easy to reverse what patriarchy has created. So far as I know and can understand matriarchal ways of thinking and Utopias, this is precisely what they do not intend, but in spite of that I see parallels. It seems to me that even here the relationship between man and woman, and now the feminine, play all too great a role. The consequences can be seen, for example, in the fact that many contemporary women who have become involved with a matriarchal spirituality have in a way over-exalted motherhood, and their being mothers, so that they have unwillingly come close to what we have already had in our culture, even if under quite different circumstances: i.e. the idolization of motherhood. It also seems that many women's groups turn in upon themselves and concentrate on their own questions. My own path takes me in another direction. Admittedly, I have learned a great deal about myself from the new women's movement and its emphasis on being a woman. I have given a great deal of attention to being a woman, to love of what is living, to relationships with the body and nature that were previously closed to me, or of which I was not so much aware. But my life-model is different, and I cannot recognize Jesus in Elga Sorge's hero; this is my main problem with her. Neither do I recognize him in the male dual system. Since Jesus is a central figure in my thinking, I must give more thought to this.

I can do this only with brief headings here. It is important to me that his call is directed to individual people, both men and women, and that it calls them into a community which is not based upon marriage and the family, as is our Church. Think of sayings such as Mark 3:35: "Whoever does the will of God is my brother, and sister, and mother." Each individual man and woman is meant here. It is a community based on "equality", which does not mean "sameness", but rather a community not based on superiority and inferiority. This is the form of Church to which we must give more thought.

Chapter 5

Women for an Inclusive Church – We Women too are Church

To END this book I want to consider the Church – that is the church(es) in their present-day form as well as the Church in which we believe and for which we hope. I recently delivered a public lecture with the title "Women for an inclusive Church". I am keeping to this title, but I have become somewhat more radical in my thinking since then. We women, that is those of us who have "broken out" and who, nevertheless, are Christians and wish to remain so, are still in favour of an inclusive Church. However, even this way of putting it gives the impression of there being a juxtaposition or distinction between "women" and "Church". This is, indeed, how we continue to experience it, but that is precisely the distortion of the true nature of the Church created and imposed by patriarchy. We need to be bolder and say: "We women too *are* Church". We are not the whole Church, as we well know, indeed only too well, which is why we need courage to use a sentence like this one: "We too *are* Church", and perhaps it takes even more courage to say: "The male-dominated Church in which we live is also Church, but it is not inclusive, it has been mutilated, it lacks the experience of half of humanity."

When I put these two ideas together in this way, it may look like a very simple matter – two separated halves that have only to find each other for everything to be solved (the old dual model of which I spoke in the last chapter). Unfortunately, however, it is not so simple. The problem of power stands between us, or, to put it more precisely: the power of patriarchy, of domination, and the subordination, not only of women to men, but also of the laity to the clergy, the poor to the rich, of nature to humanity, etc. Because this is the case, we women need a great deal of courage to say: "We too are Church", and it costs men relatively little to say: "Yes, of course we need you", while failing to work out the consequences of this, or fundamentally to question their own position – not only personally, but also collectively. Without this, all the fine words, of which there are plenty, count for nothing.

In order to make my meaning clearer when I say: "We women are Church", I turn to Elisabeth Schüssler Fiorenza again. As we have seen, she refers to the original Jesus movement, in which women were natural equals, persons, called and baptized members of the congregation with equal rights. From this fact, proved by her among others, and to my mind conclusively, she deduces that we, women and men, men and women, have a common history, a history of faith and of belonging to God in imitation of Jesus. This history has been taken over by men who have conformed congregations and Church to the dominant social structures. Officially, it is "their" history, their tradition, from which we are in effect excluded by the way the offices of the Church are confined to men, by language, by being silenced in many ways, even if it is continually said that of course we are meant to be included as well: "When we say 'brothers', the sisters are included"; and women say, as I recently heard in a Protestant church service – and the expression was a woman's – that we are called to "fraternal" service. That is the extent to which our mental colonialization has succeeded. In the face of this I say: "We are Church, and many of us have at last have had our eyes and ears opened, and we want to reclaim our history." At a conference of Catholic women in the USA in 1983 this was expressed as follows:

For the women who attended the Conference, "The Women-Church speaks", there is only one entity. Women are not in the Church; they are (the) Church. They do not claim to be the whole Church, but they do claim to be Church. Such a claim is, of course, based on the definition by the Second Vatican Council, that the Church is the people of God. What is significant here is that women appropriate this claim for themselves, as people called to a special commission in the Church and world, and this is shaped by their special experience as women.[1]

The same text says that the central problem for these women is no longer the priesthood of women, but patriarchy: "The central problem is patriarchy and its legitimation by religious language, symbols, theology and structures.... Most women believe that if the Church were to be freed from the limited outlook of patriarchy, the question of ordination would solve itself."

Since we may still be a long way from this vision, I turn now to the question of the ordination of women (briefly, as I intimated in the first chapter), and by that I mean ordination to the full priesthood. I should like to begin with the outcry of a Swiss Catholic woman who presented a petition to the Second Vatican Council on this subject. In the foreword she says:

I begin to speak as a woman of our time, who knows the needs and problems of her sisters through her studies, profession and activity over many years in the women's movement. I am turning to you (the Council Fathers) in the hope that my petition will receive the attention it deserves on account of the seriousness and weight of its content. For by giving expression to my thoughts, I feel myself to be a sister of all sisters. I should like to know that my words are understood as the complaint and accusation of half of humanity – the female half which was oppressed for thousands of years, and in whose oppression the Church, through its theory of woman, in a way that seriously wounded the Christian consciousness, was involved and is involved."[2]

---

1. Quoted in *Center of Concern* (Washington, D.C.) 58, Jan. 1984.
2. Quoted in G. Heinzelmann, *Wir schweigen nicht länger* (Zurich: Feminas Verlag, 1962).

These words speak for themselves, and I know that their implications are still being discussed in the Roman Catholic Church. But since I am better informed about the discussions in the World Council of Churches, and because these discussions illuminate the dynamics of the problem in a thoroughly comparable way, I should like to give examples from this process.

Let me start with an anecdote that describes the situation very well. In a plenary session of the World Assembly of the WCC held in Vancouver in 1983, the question was raised once again: Is the ordination of women not a hindrance to the unity of the Church? This provoked a Swiss Reformed delegate to make a heated retort, "One should not lay the burden of the question of unity on women", and she went on to ask: "Gentlemen, what were you doing for the unity of the Church before this, when there was as yet no discussion of the question of the ordination of women?"

To return to a more detailed description of the situation. The WCC study "The Community of Women and Men in the Church", from which I have already quoted, states:

> Presently, although close to one half of the WCC member churches ordain women, in terms of numbers of Christians these together do not balance the three major churches that do not, namely the Orthodox Churches, most churches of the Anglican world communion, and the Roman Catholic Church. Though the debate is essentially settled in much of Protestantism, it is almost new in the international ecumenical movement, and there is considerable resistance by some even to considering the ordination of women to the priesthood as an item for discussion.[3]

At the Sheffield Conference (1981) at which this passage was composed, it was recommended that the question should be studied further. So, in the so-called Lima Document, the Joint Declaration on Baptism, Eucharist and Ministry, which was produced by the Commission on Faith and Order of the WCC

---

3. C.F. Parvey (ed.), *The Community of Women and Men in the Church* (Geneva: WCC, 1983), p.178.

and was presented to the churches of the world (including the Roman Catholic Church) for consideration, there are two extremely carefully formulated references to this problem. I should like to quote from one of them, which is part of undoubtedly the most difficult and most controversial section on ministry:

> Where Christ is present, human barriers are being broken. The Church is called to convey to the world the image of a new humanity. There is in Christ no male or female (Gal.3:28). Both women and men must discover together their contributions to the service of Christ in the Church. The Church must discover the ministry which can be provided by women as well as that which can be provided by men. A deeper understanding of the comprehensiveness of ministry which reflects the interdependence of men and women needs to be more widely manifested in the life of the Church.
>
> Though they agree on this need, the churches draw different conclusions as to the admission of women to the ordained ministry.[4]

This passage reads as though everything can start again from the beginning, as though ministries for men as well as for women can be created anew, as though not all important church offices are *de facto* purely for men, as though there is no inequality between men and women in the structures of all churches, including those in which women can be ordained.

I do not want to bore you with further quotations of this nature. They belong to the category of well-intentioned words that serve no purpose. I prefer to sum up a debate continuing in the Anglican Church, one of the three major groups of churches referred to above. The Anglican churches in the USA and Canada ordain women, and in the mother church, the Church of England, a motion for new legislation on the admission of women to ordination was discussed in Synod in November 1984. Although a clear majority was essentially in favour, no decision was taken until November 1992, when all

---

4. *Baptism, Eucharist and Ministry* (Geneva: WCC, 1982), pp. 23–4.

three competent groups (bishops, priests and laity) approved the change with the requisite two-thirds majority. The result was welcomed with great rejoicing, especially by women, who had been waiting a long time for this outcome. When the decision is finally put into practice, women should be ordained priests of the Church of England for the first time in 1994.

It remains to be seen whether objections from Greek Orthodox quarters will have increased or diminished by then. In 1984 the Orthodox attitude was as follows:

> Under no circumstances will the Orthodox churches ignore the Apostolic tradition and the tradition of the Church Fathers, which was canonized by the Ecumenical Councils, and which upholds the claim that the special ordination for the performance and transmission of the means of divine grace, the sacraments, belongs to the male sex. . . .
>
> The so-called progressiveness of Anglicans in this question is a further unforgiveable error on the part of this Church with regard to concern for the unity of the Church. Such a step has such a negative connotation that those who are responsible should seriously consider whether the dialogue between the Orthodox and Anglicans still has any purpose."[5]

Only practice will show how the ordination of women works out, and whether it really contributes to further division in the Church. Some arguments from the 1984 discussion still apply to the whole context. In an interview, the then Archbishop of Canterbury said that personally he was in favour of the ordination of women, but nevertheless could not conceal his belief that Anglicans were duty-bound not to appear radically and unfraternally to ignore great Catholic communions with which they shared the same fundamental tenets of faith.[6] In further remarks, the ordination of women is described as a "radical change".

Are the "fundamentals of the faith" shared with one body or another really at stake here? With all due respect, this needs to be questioned: Is ecclesiology, and in particular the under-

---

5. Quoted in *Swiss Evangelical Press Service* (Zurich), 24 Feb. 1985.
6. *Church Times* (London), 23 Nov. 1984.

standing of ministry, really an essential foundation of common Christian faith? Do fundamental biblical statements like Genesis 1 on the creation of man and woman in the image of God, or Galatians 3:21, where baptism is said to break down the barriers between men and women in the Body of Christ, to give just two examples, really fade into insignificance before this? Or, to put it another way, is not the equality of man and woman, which belongs unconditionally to human beings and which is grounded in Creation, fundamental to faith? The same question arises in connection with redemption in Christ. One could also ask: Does ecclesiology take precedence over anthropology and christology?

We can only wait with concern and interest to see how things actually turn out in the Church of England. The very fact that all these processes take so long makes it all the more urgent, while pursuing the question consistently, not just to mark time but to widen the issue and to ask:

– What do women expect from the Church?
– What do women have to bring to the Church? What does the Women-Church look like?

On the subject of these expectations, I should like to quote from a young Swiss woman, who in my opinion sums up very well what many women are waiting and hoping for:

I dream of a church in which the voice of its members will be heard, in which we are aware that we, with our many problems, are understood. I dream of a church in which we women share in shaping the structures, and the decision-making, in which we do not simply conform to the existing situation. . . . In this church others no longer take action and make decisions for women. We can discuss what concerns us. In my dream this church is a true preacher of the Good News, a herald of liberation from discrimination and oppression. . . . Suddenly I awoke from my dream. A great saint who lived over four hundred years ago came to mind: Teresa of Avila, who once said: "Simply the thought that I am a woman is enough to clip my wings."

This passage comes from a speech by Elisabeth Äberli delivered during Pope John Paul II's 1984 visit to Switzerland, at his meeting with young people in Einsiedeln. It closed with the words: "Now whoever dreams, hopes."

Am I being malicious, if I place two Papal statements alongside this shy, but brave and concrete expression of hope? During his visit to Switzerland, Pope John Paul II said at a meeting with representatives of the Working Party of Christian Churches in Switzerland:

> One only has to cast a glance at Holy Scripture to recognize what a great mission belongs to women in God's act of salvation. In the old Covenant as well as in the New, women are continually called to be tools of his plan of salvation. He had need of them, and he has need of them today and tomorrow. Therefore, we have to ask ourselves seriously whether women today occupy that place in Church and society which is intended for them by the Creator and Redeemer, and whether their dignity and rights are recognized in a suitable way. These questions belong, as is well known, to the agenda of the dialogue between our churches, and we may hope that they lead to a mutual clarification and consensus of opinion.

And his predecessor Paul VI, to mark the "Year of Woman" in 1975, expressed himself in the following words: "We desire to see progress for the role of women in professions and society; the dignity and the mission of women must continue to be preserved. God has made them to be sensitive daughters, strong and pure virgins, loving wives, and especially holy and worthy mothers, and finally devout, hardworking widows."

This is simply a confirmation of the traditional roles of women. Today it is not only women who rebel against this, and so it is even more urgent to concentrate on what women mean when they say, "We are Church" and on what women can actually bring to the Church – or, to put it another way, what the Church robs itself of by hindering women from contributing their actual gifts, not to mention those that are surely still to be developed. I should like to attempt a compilation from my own experience as well as from my knowledge of what women have written on this subject. I make no claim to be comprehensive, and I should not like such a list to be made into a fixed, everlasting norm.

1. Women think differently. Women, for example, see the consequences of decisions. They see events in terms of relationships that men do not necessarily see as logical – the relationship between every living thing, but also between everything deadly: between peaceful and military technology; between violence against women and the rape of nature; between so-called small details such as verbal patriarchy and witchhunts; between the renunciation of priesthood and repressed sexuality. Women think in cycles or in spirals and not in a straight line. Linear thinking reaches its goal more quickly; cyclic thought requires time, it circles round an object. That gets on men's nerves, which then makes women speechless and helpless, because they have nothing "reasonable" to set against linear thought, which functions so logically. That is why so many contributions from women are missing from minutes of meetings and conference reports. They are incomprehensible from the "normal", i.e. masculine, viewpoint.

Women include things; they see an association; men, on the other hand, exclude things.

None of this is inborn, but learnt in different circumstances of life.

2. Women are closer to life as a consequence of their socialization. This observation, in the ecclesiastical sphere, is borne out by my experiences at the 1983 WCC World Assembly in Vancouver, where for the first time in the history of the ecumenical movement, perhaps for the first time since the Jesus movement, women comprised, not indeed half the participants in an official worldwide church forum, but at least about one third, and not only of the accredited, voting delegates, but also of those speaking, the leaders, and so on.

What was their contribution? First of all, the conference was more colourful, warmer, more lively, more down-to-earth, more original than other conferences – actually even more spiritual. For me it corresponded to the image of a participatory church far more than previous World Assemblies. But I should like to go a step further. When I re-read the theological contributions made by women, what strikes me is that basic experiences of women were expressed in a way I had never heard before. The theme was "Jesus Christ, the Life of the World". What could be more natural than to use the image of birth? Jesus himself did this when he said, in John 16:21: "When a woman is in travail, she has sorrow because her hour is come, but when she is delivered of the child, she no longer remembers the anguish for joy that a human being is born into the world." Jesus uses this metaphor for the situation of his disciples, whom he is leaving alone, unhappy, in pain. In Vancouver the phrase was used many times by women: waiting for the time when the child is born. Cramps and pain until it comes into the world – images for faith, images true to life. I should like to give one more example, quoted verbatim. A woman gave the sermon at the opening service. Among other things she spoke of the martyrs of our age, of those who had lost their lives for the sake of their faith since the last world assembly, such as Archbishop Romero of San Salvador, and then she said:

> The spilling of blood not only signifies destruction and death, it can also be a symbol for creation and life. For a woman it is a sign that her body is in a position to give birth, that new life exists in her. And also, if she herself does not experience the privilege of motherhood, instincts and energies that are released in her can be used by God in that he allows her to take part in the preservation and nurture of his children, above all, of those who are humiliated, deprived of their rights, or robbed of their full dignity as human beings. We live in a world which carries within it the coming of his Kingdom. We share in the labour pains and the sweat through which the new age of the Son of God is brought into the world.

There were further similar texts, but I must limit myself. Common to all was their not defining a purely spiritual rebirth. Even when women who had had no children themselves spoke, something of women's typical experience was conveyed in their words, brought into the Church. Perhaps some found it a stumbling block to hear the blood of the martyrs, the blood of Christ, and the blood of completely normal women being so closely associated. For many of us it was endlessly liberating. Our physical nature has been under a taboo in the Church for so long, and is still so, even today! "A pregnant woman in the pulpit, or at the altar? Impossible!" This is something one still hears today.

What do we women have to contribute? Being true to life, concern for life, overcoming the division of spirit and body (which we have never understood), a new affirmation of our bodily nature, and also our form of sexuality, another, concrete way of thinking, the ability to say "I" instead of proclaiming so-called objective eternal truths. Perhaps we also contribute a new view of sin and redemption. We are not those who storm the heavens, who raise themselves up, who reach for the stars, who must first be brought low before they can lift themselves up. Rather we are those who miss out on life through lack of self-esteem, self-denigration and misplaced modesty. We recognize ourselves in the crippled woman who was healed by Jesus, and stood upright. On the other hand, we also bring joy in life, and love of life, of life that God has created. In Genesis 3:20, Eve has a fantastic name. She is called the mother of all living things. We should like to reclaim this name for ourselves, to be not "the gateway to sin", but the mother of all living things. This goes far beyond the so-called "question of women". To a growing extent we feel responsible for Creation, which has been destroyed by us humans. Together with men, we feel that we are committed, and with a particular emphasis for life and against death, against the futility of armaments, against alleged security, against a meaningless technocracy, against the domination of economic thinking. We not only want to be liberated ourselves, but we fight for the liberation of all the oppressed, such as the minorities among us and the people of the Third World. We do that together with men, but we hope that in the struggle for the life of creation, justice, freedom and peace, men also perceive our oppression, and do not turn into oppressors of women afresh. As Christian feminists, we understand this process of liberation as liberation in the power of divine love. We hope for a Church that does not reject everything, that gives us time and space to think through in our own way what is instinctively there, to allow it to mature, without a brake being applied to this approach by rash recall and anxious admonition – and without our becoming so radicalized that communication is no longer possible.

3. Women are today readier than most men to make a connection between their own entirely personal experience and major world problems. Here is yet another illustration from Vancouver. Speaking on the theme of Justice and Peace, an Indian woman, Aruna Gnanadason, described her experiences and her insights in a story and a metaphor. She told a story, because stories pass on the message of courage and hope better than theoretical treatment. Here is an extract:

> The "Chipko" movement was organized by rural women in northern India, in order to protect their forests, their livelihood, their sustenance and their life. When the power saws arrived to fell their trees, each woman put her arms round a tree to protect it, ready to risk her life. "Chipko" means "to embrace". It was the slogan for the demand of the women of an entire tribe for life in all its fullness. The struggle of these women was directed against the "Beast", the monster, which decrees what is done with the resources of the world, land, capital, human labour and even the human spirit.

Aruna then described where and how this monster manifests itself in concrete form, and drew the conclusion that there must be the same commitment on the part of the Christian churches in the struggle against injustice and violence, and for life and peace: "From our own experience of life as women, we know that endangered human relations between partners can be healed if one of the two dares to take the first step towards reconciliation. That is also true in politics and in conflict between nations. The churches are therefore called to give their support to the first step towards reconciliation and disarmament."

This call evoked little support. Some subtle theologians wanted to know whether the Beast was identical with the "Beast from the pit" of the Apocalypse. Others saw relationships they assumed to be complicated and complex being oversimplified in the metaphor of the Beast. You can't do that – transfer very naive experiences from one sphere, that of Indian rural women, into another, that of the Church's activity, from the personal into the political! Yet one sensed loving and suffering – or at any rate I sensed these – behind the words of this woman. Are only analytical ways of thinking admissible in working sessions whose subjects are pre-set, and which are still shaped by a majority made up of men? The parallel with what happened to the women on the first Easter morning and later in the history of the Church is obvious.

What would become of our churches, if they really took women's experiences seriously? And then, not only women's experiences, but also the experiences of all those others who are condemned to silence, to loss of speech?

I want to end this book by examining two texts from the New Testament, one of which has stayed with me throughout the whole of my life, while the other has become increasingly important to me in recent years. I shall begin with the second, Mark 10:42–5:

> And Jesus called them to him and said to them, "You know that those who are supposed to rule over the Gentiles lord it over them, and their great men exercise authority over them. But it is not so among you; but whoever would be great among you must be your servant, and whoever would be first among you must be slave of all. For the Son of man also came not to be served but to serve, and to give his life as a ransom for many."

This passage is preceded by something very simple. Two of the disciples sought a privilege; they wanted the seats of honour at Jesus' side "in his glory". Jesus told them that his way was not an easy way, that they must share his suffering, and that it was not in his power to promise them such places. Then there follow the sentences I have just quoted. The story continues in a very human way. The other disciples get annoyed with the two who want to grab the places of honour. Presumably they too would have liked to have these places. Jesus tries to explain to them that they have not understood what his purpose is at all, namely, the establishment of a community that abides by other laws. The former community is the one that goes its way in "the world", where "those who are supposed to be the lords of the peoples, exercise lordship over them. . . ." [Literal translation into English of a German translation by E. Schweizer, which uses "lord" twice.] We know many forms of such lordship, or domination. In this book it is always seen in connection with patriarchy, with being "lord" in the literal sense of the word, which does not mean that the world is to be interpreted monocausally. However that may be, what is clear is Jesus' direction or comment, "But it is not so among you." Not "it must not (or even – it should not) be so among you", but "it is not so." Jesus places those whom he calls in a new kind of community, also (as Elisabeth Schüssler Fiorenza points out) in a new kind of legitimacy. He designates this community with a word that for many of us has been overloaded with problems, the word "serve". This is a particularly difficult word for us women. We are, indeed, always being told to serve: "Let the wife learn to serve as is her destiny" (Goethe) – serve in the home, in the family, in the Church, everywhere. I keep asking myself why this word has become so difficult for us. Precisely because in our tradition to "serve" means in actual fact to fit in with the stronger. It suggests a servile sort of following, not the "following after" Jesus, or discipleship, which in his time was something very non-conformist, independent, requiring a decision to leave everything, the decision of exodus. "Following" has become associated with submission, bowing to the will of another, breaking one's own will. Of course it then meant submission to the will of God, but in the Church this was usually represented by the will of some "Father" or "Lord". Theoretically, of course, these derived their authority from God, but in practice they fashioned God's image in accordance with their own.

For all these reasons I still have trouble with the word "serve". It goes against the grain with me particularly because the exploitation of every form of service, especially where we women are concerned, is so obvious. And Jesus appears to confirm this, but this is only a superficial impression. Jesus is speaking on this particular occasion to his closest circle of disciples, who were men. For me, the word "serve" loses much of its difficulty when it is addressed to men and women, and I find it easier to put aside the old clichés still embedded in me when I realize that Jesus understood his own way as one of service. This way was definitely not one of conformity. He was not obedient. He did not observe the rules of the society in which he lived. He did not want to be king, as his disciples would gladly have made him. His entry into Jerusalem was basically a very modest one.

Perhaps we should remember a few stories from his life. Elisabeth Schüssler Fiorenza has pointed out that the Synoptic tradition says seven times that the first should be last and the last (slaves and women, who were put on the same level) first. The most famous story is Mark 9:36, where Jesus placed a child in the midst of his disciples, who had been arguing with each other about who was the greatest. But there are other examples also. Jesus enjoyed table fellowship with very different people: he ate with the rich but also incurred their anger (and that of his disciples) when a woman – and a known sinner to boot – anointed him (Luke 7:37). He sat at the table of the rich, but as a free man.

In the community he built, there was a place not only for the despised tax-collectors and the disciples who came from the lower strata of society, but also for women, who were on the margins of society, whose words counted for nothing. However, it was not simply a matter of reversing existing relationships; barriers fell away between those who followed Jesus the wandering preacher, or who received him into their houses, such as Martha and Mary.

This form of congregation changed very quickly in the early church, and conformed to the dominant relationships. But it is precisely for this reason that it is important to read texts such as these, to learn new things from them. Perhaps doing so will give us a new understanding of Jesus' death as the logical outcome of a course that takes no thought for itself. Jesus expects those who follow him to take this risk also. Why this risk? Because, I believe, a community that in principle rejects the necessity of domination is provocative, dangerous. It is, in fact, a community of mutual love, one that takes everyone seriously, the weak and the strong. But if what is generally accepted is called into question, if the existing relations of power and subordination – even between men and women – are questioned (by participation, the right of everyone at all levels to speak), then things begin to shake. Then the world takes on a different appearance.

Now, it can of course be said: "That applies only within the congregation, or even only in the Kingdom of God." I don't believe this. I believe that if we were to set out upon this way seriously, if our congregations really sought ways to include everyone (I know this would be a long and difficult way, and one perhaps never to be completed), then it would spread, it would be infectious. And people would think that something like this should be possible, not only in the Church, but also in other spheres – in business, in politics, in environmental protection. Up to now, only experts have had the right to speak. All those affected need to be able to participate, not merely to be heard. This is the only way for trust to grow among all people.

The second text is Galatians 3:26–8: "For in Christ Jesus you are all sons of God, through faith. For as many of you as were baptized into Christ have put on Christ. There is neither Jew nor Greek, there is neither slave nor free, there is neither male nor female; for you are all one in Christ Jesus."

This has been one of the guiding texts of my life. Obviously, it is the statement about "male" and "female" that concerned me most, but the context too was important. This text is found in virtually all theological books written by women. For many of us, it has meant recognition in the face of our under-valuation in the Church, and it provides recognition from the Bible. It has helped with the problems of life, given a sense of direction, moved into a new reality, and moreover all this comes in the context of a letter dealing with freedom: "For you were called to freedom" (Gal. 5:13), and in which Paul passionately fights against the congregation he founded falling back into old, outworn structures (Gal. 3:1; 5:2; 6:12).

The assumption underlying the sentence that concerned us most was, "You are all children (in the Greek, "sons") of God through faith, and have put on Christ in baptism" – you have been placed in a new reality. Today many scholars accept that this verse comes from an old baptismal formula, which Paul took over. However that may be, what did the new reality consists of? Three forms of domination and subordination, of inclusion and exclusion, are named:

– Jew-Greek
– Slave-free
– Male-female (the same words as in Genesis 1)

In the community created by Jesus, the barriers between these groups of people are lifted; all together form the Body of Christ.

This again raises the vital question: Does this apply only "before God" or also in the real world of Church and society? Many commentaries claim that it applies only "before God", and that it will only become reality in the (eschatological) Kingdom of God, so it is not permissible to draw conclusions for our life today. I regard this as a diminishing and falsification of biblical assertions, and believe we should take seriously the lifting of all barriers and our belonging together in the Body of Christ, with all its consequences for the Church and the structuring of society.

Then it would be seen that the Bible contains passages that possess an explosive power – a power by no means exhausted yet – and some part of this power would be released.

Perhaps we women, the "Women-Church", can help in this respect. From our experience we know something of mutuality, of having to be strong and weak in turn, of changing authorities, of relying on one another, of accepting and taking each other seriously, of listening, of being left alone and still carrying on. How long will the church of men take to move towards structures free of domination? We cannot return to the forms of the primitive church, even if we need them as a model and vision, but we can move forwards into a sisterly, brotherly, human community, a church of liberation and of full humanity for all. I do not give up the hope that Jesus, with the power of his love, and the community of the Sophia/Spirit are with us, and that even patriarchs can learn to do without power and violence, because they no longer find it necessary to assert themselves in this way.

POSTSCRIPT

The Church of England's Decision to ordain Women to the Priesthood

FOR THE TV cameras, it made a perfect closing shot: "RC women next". I refer to the banner held outside Church House, Westminster, on 11 November 1992. As the champagne corks began to pop and jubilant singing filled the evening air after the results of the vote on the ordination of women were announced, a hand-written slogan was held up in full view by a group of the Roman Catholics who were there. As the cameras ended their filming for the Six o'clock TV News one set of Catholic aspirations was clear: "RC women next".

The image is recorded on film; it is also recorded in the consciousness of Catholic women everywhere. Something of inestimable importance for all women was done on that day. A Church which declares itself to be in the apostolic tradition has demonstrated its conviction that women are inextricably caught into the saving mysteries of Christ's incarnation, passion, death and resurrection from the dead. No longer is the Eucharist something that will be done to us or done on our behalf, cloaked in euphemisms about the integrity of the whole worshipping community. We will be the subjects as well as the objects of our eucharistic destiny.

I write this postscript to Marga Bührig's book in the month following the vote. Already the ecumenical world is configured in different ways; the end of the story has yet to be told. What I offer here is a snapshot, a prediction of where the new ecumenical faultlines now fall and what this is likely to mean for the Christian imagination in the years to come.

I detect signs of three faultlines. There may well be more. And of course they are not brand new, they have been stretching and straining for attention for a long time now. The first relates to the place of women in Church and society. Christian opinion is now publicly split. For over one hundred

123

years women have been receiving an education as demanding
and all-embracing as their male counterparts. And this
education has been given in Christian schools as an integral
part of the Christian endeavour. No wonder then that many
women are baffled when the aspirations they have legiti-
mately acquired along with their education are dismissed in
the name of a "proper dignity" based in an outmoded biology
or genetic naivety. The old order no longer works; and to many
Christian women it seems little less than tragic that Christian
men close doors to them in the name of a gospel which claims
to bring good news to both.

Yet Christian opinion is divided and the faultline is now
wide open as never before. Angry voices are raised around the
place where it gapes. The more vociferous slag each other off,
as "a virus in the bloodstream of the universal Church"
(Graham Leonard, former Bishop of London, in a General
Synod Debate in 1987) or, contrariwise, as misogynists bent on
institutionalizing sexism. The more moderate note that any
bastion of male power has found it extraordinarily difficult to
share this power. Every profession that has been closed to
women has enjoyed high status. And once open to women the
status goes down. Medicine and teaching are obvious
examples.

This moderate voice also seeks to raise questions about the
renewal of ministry in general, as well as the ordination of
women in particular. Given the extraordinarily complexity of
pastoral need at the moment, how is ministry to be renewed in
a way which will meet the spiritual and emotional life of the
average worshipper? How can we reach down into the mud of
many people's lives and remind them of the existence of the
stars? Let alone of the fact that God's original creative act
began in mud – when most have never laid their hand on a
Bible and are ignorant of its most basic contents, let alone its
themes?

This yawning gap divides in new and deeply-fraught ways.
It creates new alliances. Scriptural fundamentalists, tightly-
corsetted women from the white Tory highlands and the black-
suited clergy make slightly comic bed fellows, but that is what
they have become. On the other hand, liberals and radicals and

women in the pew – as well as on the bench, at the bar and the university rostrum who have not darkened a church door since their wedding day – all are welded into a new "right-on" consortium of indignation.

Reconciliation between the two will be hard. And ironically one way of achieving it may well be for the Roman Catholic Church to get on and ordain women, so removing some of the sting and acrimony from the arguments used by both sides.

Then of course there is the whole question of Catholicity. Here a new faultline looms in the imagination of the English Catholic community, whether Roman or Anglo-Catholic. Newman's option of going over to Rome was somehow more do-able in the nineteenth century. Now that the Roman Church has had its Second Vatican Council, its drawing power is diminished. Whereas the First Vatican Council was a totally different matter; an ultra-montane English Catholic community might have welcomed the arrival of smart hordes from the Established Church. Together both could have fixed their gaze on Rome. Present-day Roman Catholics are more choosy. Judging by the letters in the press over the past month, they seek to discourage any attempts to (in the jargon) "cross the Tiber", for the simple reason that they dislike and mistrust the Catholicity of a group of clergy and lay people who appear to seek to "convert on the rebound".

Nevertheless, there is a major question here. While it is important to know the history – and so important for Anglo-Catholics to remember that RCs cannot forget the legacy of the Reformation in too much of a hurry – there is an agenda for reconciliation here as well. How can the word Catholic be reclaimed? How can it speak to a contemporary quest for all that is one, true, holy and apostolic? Where do these marks of fidelity lie? What is it to be Catholic nowadays? And how can this Catholicity be set in place without automatically excluding the heirs of the Reformation in all our Churches?

While questions such as these preoccupy official church people and the staffs of ecumenical instruments like the Council of Churches for Britain and Ireland where I work, it would be naive to assume that this is the beginning and end of the question, especially the question of ecumenism. What the ordination of women debate in the Church of England has revealed to me is that there is a range of ecumenical activity already up and running, about which the mainstream Churches know nothing.

In ordinary homes this brings people together in inter-church marriages. In women's groups it brings them together to make theology. In informal ecumenical networks it brings them together in friendship and social action. While Church Councils struggle to find the right formulae, make the right noises and receive the right delegations, Christian people are meeting and loving and working together as never before. And women are at the sharp end of many of these encounters. While they may not always have celebrated eucharists together, they have blessed each other's new homes, they have held seders or summer picnics. Above all they have found an authentic and authoritative voice in which to speak of the great things that God has done for them. Women such as these want the ministry of women to grow. They know what it looks like in both its ordained and its unordained forms, and they want more of it.

Indeed, as they see it, this hidden part of the ecumenical journey of the Churches in England, Ireland, Scotland and Wales now deserves to come into the light and to feed the public discourse of ecumenism. So here too reconciliation is needed. And here too the Churches have nothing to lose and everything to gain. So who will be the ministers who can bring this hidden tradition into the light? Arguably the ordained women in ALL our Churches. A true renewal of ministry would empower them all – and do so without disempowering the rest of us.

Lavinia Byrne IBVM
Associate Secretary for the Community of Women and Men in the Church at the Council of Churches for Britain and Ireland